DEDICATION

"If a man does not keep pace with his companions, perhaps it is because he hears a different drummer.
Let him step to the music which he hears,
however measured or far away."
- Henry David Thoreau

I would like to dedicate this work to two individuals, who, have meant everything to my life: My mother and my wife. I am listing them in this order because my mother started me on my journey through life and my wife is at my side as we enter our twilight years.

My mother, Edith Waterman Ward, taught me to question everything, to cuss and discuss anything I didn't understand, and to search for the less obvious answers. "Thinking outside the box" is a popular saying but in my family, it was expected. I cannot enter into a discussion without remembering something my mother once told me: When a high school teacher was finally dismissed; two years after I quit the class and told my mother I wouldn't return, my mother said to me, "It will do you no good to be right two years ahead of everyone else." I only wish I had followed her insight throughout my life.

My wife, Peggy Janet Talley Ward, has stood by my side when I undoubtedly made her life miserable. She has supported me in battle after battle and smiled when people asked her, "How can you live with that man?" Most of all, she has always given me unconditional love, when I most needed support, and has shown an almost irrational faith in my ability to succeed. Many of the lessons I have learned over the years are contained within this book. I would never have experienced these without the certainty that she was there to support me.

A Grumpy Old Man
on Education

Lawrence "Alan" Ward

with Musings and Editing by Alexys Akey

Copyright © 2016 Lawrence "Alan" Ward

ISBN-13: 978-0692630341
ISBN-10: 0692630341

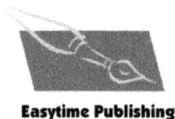

Easytime Publishing

Easytime Publishing
Lake Havasu City, AZ.
www.EasytimePublishing.com

PREFACE

"We must never forget that the educational system is essentially a monopoly; and as such it will strive to deliver an inferior product at an exorbitant price. Only a stern and consistent review of policies and procedures can harness this tendency."

- Ward

This has long been an ambition of mine. As I have gotten older, I have become more and more convinced this type of work has a place today. One of the most frustrating things individuals face as they age, is the fact that the same mistakes are still being made which they faced and remedied years earlier.

If you continue to read this, you will notice that I am not attempting to present a work supported by a plethora of quantitative studies. While I will occasionally cite a study, in most cases, I will merely provide an observation and pose questions that I perceive as pertinent. In today's world, we often become transfixed on the concept that all "valuable" academic work "must" be legitimized with some form of published study. We squash originality as we spent most of our time generating data sets for the sake of generating data sets. I will not attempt to do this. This will be an anecdotal work, which will, at times, resemble a person's breath - it may seem to stink to many of you. If you do decide to read on, I hope you gain some insights that, whether you agree with them or not, will cause you to reconsider your current perspectives.

Saying this, it is to be noted that a generation of astute graduate students can anchor their careers by generating data sets to either prove or disprove these observations. I am sure that those refuting my observations will meet with wide spread approval within the established world of educational academics. Those finding agreement can then publish in rebuttal. In this way, I may well serve a purpose in furthering the knowledge of one or more disciplines. It may at least propel some dedicated graduate student to tenure through publication.

Having taught at the university, community college, and high school levels. I feel that many of these observations may lend themselves to reflections resulting in an improved system of education within the United States. These will, at least, stimulate a fresh discussion of many issues that should lead to renewed interest and potential improvements.

It is very important for me to provide you with some healthy advice. As you peruse this work, you will develop a sense of negativity and potential hostility. We must keep in mind the fact that tens of thousands of deeply dedicated and courageous individuals serve our children every day. We call these wonderful and sacrificing people our educators. A work like this is not intended to detract from their efforts, however, its intent is to force us to examine those things that are causing those valiant efforts to deliver a less than acceptable result. My advice is to take this work in small bites and then, reflect on how simple the solutions are to many of these issues.

For those teaching professionals who may be offended by any observations I may make; please understand that I am providing these to encourage you to reflect on the paradigms, which have driven your profession.

For those administrators who will most assuredly be offended: I must suggest that you could gain much by contemplating if these observations apply to yourself or to any of your associates. If they do, then the question becomes: what will you do to correct them?

For my family, friends, and loved ones: I deeply hope that this work will not cause you to be embarrassed by my frankness and lack of political correctness.

"The traditional educational theory is to the effect that the way to bring up children is to keep them innocent, in other words, believing in biological, political, and socio-economic fairy tales, as long as possible... That students should be given the best possible maps of the territories of experience in order that they may be prepared for life, is not as popular as might be assumed."
- S.I. Hayakawa

ISSUES ADDRESSED

CHAPTER 1: The Singular Paradigm

CHAPTER 2: Professional Incest

CHAPTER 3: "Look-me-ups" - Technology and
the Modern Student

CHAPTER 4: Evaluations/progress/drop outs

CHAPTER 5: Classroom Segregation

CHAPTER 6: Curriculum Structure

CHAPTER 7: Educational Funding

CHAPTER 8: Parents/Communities/Public Relations

CHAPTER 9: Culture, Teachers, Students

CHAPTER 10: Program Management

CHAPTER 11: WHY??

CHAPTER 12: Summary and Suggestions

Chapter 1
The Singular Paradigm

"After you've done a thing the same way for two years, look it over carefully. After five years, look at it with suspicion. And after ten years, throw it away and start over."
- Alfred Edward Perlman

JUAN: I'd like to start with the story of Juan. When I first began to teach, I encountered a junior in high school, who we will call "Juan." I am changing his name for this story. Juan was a very personable young man. He was not a legal resident and appeared rather bright. The problem was that Juan was often disruptive and didn't do well on tests. It reached a point where I called him out to the hallway and the exchange went as follows:

Me: "Juan, you are going to get me fired."

Juan: "Why, Mr. Ward?"

Me: "Because you won't behave. But let me tell you: the only way you will know is that you will read about it from your hospital bed. Now, get back in that classroom, shut up, and do your work."

Juan became my strongest supporter but still there was the test problem. I found if I read the questions, he could achieve very good grades – B's or C's. My first inclination was that he couldn't read English. He was attending ESL (English as a Second Language) classes. However, his ESL teacher told me he was only interested in the girls and not in learning English. I continued to watch him and often, would explain a chapter's lessons. He became a model student, but still failed the tests.

Then, one day, a young Hispanic girl came to me between classes and asked me if she could tell me something in confidence. Agreeing, I listened as she told me that Juan couldn't read ANY language. She asked for anonymity because Juan was so ashamed.

I quickly informed the ESL teacher, after several meetings we got Juan to agree to private reading lessons. Juan later joined the Marine Corps and, to my knowledge, is doing well.

Why do I start with this story? I want everyone reading this to ask themselves if they are addressing our educational problems at the institutional level **AND** the individual level from a preconceived notion of the problem. You see, because Juan was Hispanic, and obviously bright, he had been socially promoted under the assumption that he couldn't read English.

As you read I will ask you to remember Juan and consider the problems I choose to address from the viewpoint of asking yourself: What is the REAL problem?

In both the university setting and the community college classroom, I was appalled at the lack of preparation our freshmen students had. Later, as I worked toward my "alternative" certification and began to teach at the high school level, I became aware of a phenomenon that is crippling our students: One I have named the "Kiddo syndrome", that I believe is at the crux of the continued degeneration of our education system.

While pursuing my certification, I noted that virtually every presenter would continually address the students as "kiddos." This was, at first, mildly irritating to an old retired Marine - which slowly led to what I consider an epiphany.

Having served in Vietnam and worked alongside 17 and 18 year-old Marines, requiring them to be adults, I realized that our graduates were still considered "kids." They were being treated as kids and we were expecting them to perform and submit work that was reflective of our view of them as kids. When coupled with many of the other influencing variables, this makes it difficult for any teacher to expect higher outcomes much less demand them.

We are now becoming trapped in a paradigm that extends from elementary school to intermediate school and into high school. This paradigm is corrosive to the educational development of our younger generations. Class after class progresses through the system with no concentrated effort to develop their maturity and academic discipline.

Sadly, the perpetrators of this crime are the most well intentioned. I've heard teachers and parents state that they didn't like taking notes in school and are grateful that their child isn't required to do that "unnecessary work." Or, that they feel reciting multiplication tables or reading aloud is too much of a strain on their child's psyche. Question: How did these adults get so well educated doing these things if they served no purpose???

ELEMENTARY SCHOOL: Let's break down the issue by looking at our bright young student "Johnny." Johnny enters grade school at a point of development that requires interesting and stimulating activities to maintain his attention. Without these activities, Johnny won't pay attention or concentrate on the material we wish him to learn. As a result, we construct group activities, films, educational games, and any other form of entertaining educational activities we can develop.

Johnny begins to learn he can avoid the foundational material he will need later in his academic development. We also take almost maniacal care not to alienate Johnny by making education too demanding. Making him read aloud might embarrass him. Asking him to recite his multiplication tables might also turn him off. Well, Johnny flies through elementary school and "graduates" to intermediate school.

In addition, Johnny receives awards for the following: On time to class, well behaved, a neat desk, his shoes are tied, he ate his entire lunch, and he didn't wet his pants. Of course, I'm saying this tongue in cheek. I once watched a teacher make hundreds of awards for a grade school class so students wouldn't be "left out." Now, while I agree we shouldn't purposefully exclude students, we also should not make them feel that being a loser is winning. They need to begin learning that there are winners and losers and most of the time it relates to the effort expended.

Unfortunately, the skills (not the facts) learned at this level, will affect Johnny's entire success in education. Without a firm foundation in proper academic student skills focused on how to be a successful student, the facts we expose Johnny to will yield little long-range educational benefit, even if they are entertaining. While I believe in some forms of systematic testing, we must make sure that facts alone are not our focus.

INTERMEDIATE SCHOOL: Heeere's Johnny!!! Now entering intermediate school, Johnny is just beginning to feel the raging hormones that will make every day an adventure. The problem now is that our system has accepted that the mode of instruction should be entertaining and fun. Article after article expounds on the idea the children learn more when they "enjoy" the experience. So, we transfer the same paradigm we were using in elementary school to intermediate school and continue to believe that, at this new maturity level, Johnny's level of concentration is so poor that we must keep him involved and we require the teacher to provide varied stimulating lessons. In fact, we repeatedly tell the teachers that, if Johnny isn't learning, the teacher should change their methods or investigate other intervention techniques. Parents tell teachers that if Johnny isn't learning, it is the teachers fault and administrators' support that view.

Teachers are taught, and it is reinforced in staff development, that children have different learning styles. Correct or not, the teachers then presume that they must ensure every form of learning experience is available to the student. Understand, "kiddos" aren't stupid. They quickly learn that they can say the magic words. I faced a situation where I had a junior in high school tell me, "Mr. Ward I can't learn this way. I'm a visual learner. Can't we watch a film?" As a result, teachers often spend almost as much time developing "stimulating" lessons as they do teaching the material. It begins to become difficult for teachers to discern the difference between "being an effective teacher" and "being able to develop striking and impressive lessons."

At this point, we still haven't addressed the fact that Johnny will need to, at some point, **learn how to learn**. Johnny still hasn't had to read or recite in class if he claims it embarrasses him. The students quickly learn this is a way to get alternative assignments. Textbooks and note taking are considered "too restrictive." So, Johnny hasn't learned the fundamentals needed to gain knowledge on his own. This places the teacher under more and more pressure to attempt to entertain so that Johnny will retain at least part of the material.

To complicate the issue even further, Johnny has learned that if his grades are failing and he is interviewed, he can claim that the instruction is boring or too hard. This will almost always get Johnny a class change to a "more stimulating" class with a teacher who doesn't have a "personality clash" with poor Johnny.

To this point, no one has forced Johnny to develop his learning skills. Those students with parents concerned enough will learn these skills from their parents the others will proceed without them. Johnny is "graduating" to high school.

We are now beginning to "identify" or, "profile" the students we consider to be "gifted." These are usually the students that have parents who insist they apply themselves. Rarely do they meet the standard of the mentally gifted. We have now developed a system of discrimination based upon conduct and academic maturity, which allows the less troublesome students to be segregated from the "level" students. Now, Johnny is either one of the elite, who gets special treatment and becomes isolated from "them" or is one of "them" and is only influenced by the most disruptive and least academically capable of students. In one school, I personally witnessed the "good" students being invited to eat their lunch in the classroom with the teacher, while all the "level" students ate in the cafeteria with the rest of the "mob."

Unfortunately, this segregation often results in the worst of both worlds. The "gifted" students become dragged backward by those whose parents won't accept their children aren't "gifted." The "level" students fail to excel in part because they experience no peer pressure to succeed and teachers who don't expect them to meet the advanced standards. But, Johnny has survived and we will socially promote him to the next level.

I once had a principal from an intermediate school ask me if 90% of my students got A's or B's. When I said no, I was advised that I would never work for that individual. Gratefully, I never was placed in the position where I might be so unlikely to need to work for an administrator so concerned with outcome "appearances" and not on student development. So, Johnny, without any true learning skills and already identified as gifted or normal, will now proceed to the next step in his journey toward mediocrity.

HIGH SCHOOL: Oh boy! We have a new batch of "kiddos" arriving to their freshman year at "We're the Greatest High School." They are on the last leg of their educational preparation to join the world of academia or proceed to earn a skill that will make them productive members of society.

Johnny quickly finds out that the teachers at the high school level are overwhelmed. The teachers now have students that would-be adults in any other nation; with many of them raising their own families and working for a living. The problem is that the teachers still believe that they must entertain the students to make education a stimulating experience or the Johnny's of this world won't learn.

The first year I taught at the high school level I was amazed to find a sophomore class sitting in the hallway working on a "project." Everyone was commenting on how well they were doing and you would have thought that they were learning. The project was to individually draw an original heraldic shield, color it, and post it in the classroom. This "project" lasted for one entire week of instruction. These were young adults, whose minds are an empty pitcher, but instead of learning, they were playing. I asked the teacher if the concept of a heraldic shield couldn't be taught in 30 minutes and was told that they needed stimulation to learn.

I propose that what we did was transferred the need for young grade school children to be stimulated to the high school level and, as a result, have retarded the students' ability to apply themselves and learn. Five days were spent in this effort. The children were encouraged to expect entertainment and, even more insidiously, the teacher felt it was justified and the administration stopped by to "ooh and aah" over the students' efforts. The students weren't learning any new material and the teacher was being lauded and reinforced into thinking something had been achieved. No one mentioned the fact that this might have been appropriate for an art class but not for a world history class.

As a result of the "kiddo" paradigm, Johnny still hasn't learned the basics of becoming a scholar. Many schools set no standard requirement for notebooks, so Johnny may or may not face a teacher who will take the time to teach him how to take notes and use them in conjunction with his text to learn. Textbooks are expensive, so instead of directing funds toward books, schools are progressively moving toward on-line texts (will be discussed later). As a result, Johnny doesn't learn how to use a text for anything other than a reference that is available on-line. Reading the text, then comparing notes, lectures, and text, is becoming a lost art that will now have to be taught at the freshman level of college. Johnny will often drop out or fail in his freshman year of college. While he is very capable mentally, he is woefully academically and emotionally unprepared because upper education is not about entertainment.

SOLUTIONS: Let's understand, none of these issues apply universally but they are wide spread. The solutions are sometimes extremely complicated but, at other times, they are much more a matter of recognizing the issues and addressing them.

To address the "kiddo" paradigm, we first need to recognize that our children are progressing through three totally separate levels of academic maturity, closely related to their physical and emotional maturity. After all, that's why we developed an elementary, intermediate, and high school system. As a result, we must begin to examine the basic structure of our educational methodology as separate entities, which not only provide stimulating lessons, but also provide for the development of academic tools that will ensure success at the next level.

A good example of this type of development is the AVID (**A**dvancement **V**ia **I**ndividual **D**etermination) program. It teaches students how to formulate notes using the Cornell note-taking system. The problem is that, in most cases, it is only applied to a limited population (usually Advanced Placement students - you know those students whose parents care and who would have succeeded without special attention). Our system constantly reverts to the "academic freedom" argument when these issues are addressed. In fact, this note taking system should be initiated and it should be required of all teachers to establish some form of note grading process, beginning in the intermediate school. Nothing about this would infringe on a teachers "academic freedom" but it would force students to develop a critical tool for future academic success.

Intermediate level teachers need to insist on students reading aloud and reciting their knowledge to the class. They also need to teach students how to use their notes and texts to gain and learn from the synergy between the two. The idea that "kiddos" need a teacher to develop lessons to stimulate every sense must be reexamined. Johnny is beginning to enter the level of maturity where he can experience these senses from memory. E.g. I will challenge every reader to open an unillustrated pornography paperback. I will bet you can visualize the events, often are physically stimulated, and even imagine the sounds and smells. Well, Johnny is beginning to develop a foundation of knowledge that will allow him/her to visualize a battle, imagine the pain of a broken bone, feel the agony of losing a pet, etc. We are beginning to enter a phase where Johnny must adapt to the teacher instead of the teacher adapting to Johnny. Now, don't misunderstand - I am not saying that the teacher shouldn't make every effort to help those students that are having problems by using alternative techniques. I am saying that, at this stage, the teacher has to begin expecting Johnny to adapt, unless unusual circumstances occur.

It is also at the intermediate level where we must begin a concentrated public relations program to assist the community to recognize the goals of education. This is the point where a transition must be made from "it's the teacher's responsibility to ensure Johnny learns" to "Johnny must apply himself." Now, that's not to say that teachers shouldn't be held responsible for their actions and attention to their profession, but that a gradual shift toward Johnny's responsibilities in the educational dynamic is imperative. We must form relationships with parents so this transition can be made. I often listened to parents who believed every failure is the systems responsibility. One parent said to me: "It's your job to see to it that my son doesn't fail."

Johnny should begin being held responsible for the things which are currently **"not allowed to be graded."** Neat assignments, on time submissions, original submissions, etc. Life grades the ability to follow directions. Why shouldn't our education system? Success will depend on their ability to perform as directed.

At the high school level, written work has to be encouraged at every level. Standard work submissions need to be emphasized so students understand that their work must meet expectations. Cover pages, paper headings, ink color, submission deadlines etc. should be school standards not "at the option of the teacher."

I once had one of the finest teachers I ever knew tell me that they couldn't see any reason to demand that a student have notes. They hated notes and they had succeeded very well and wouldn't demand note taking of their students. I asked them if they had taken notes in college and their answer was, "Of course. There was too much material to learn in class." So, what are we doing? We are limiting Johnny's ability to be successful and reducing the load in class so notes aren't necessary.

What about the students' responsibility to complete homework? Well, let's stop kidding ourselves that homework teaches students. When you went to high school you never faced the volume of homework our teachers are trying to get students to perform as they **try to cram facts** into their heads.

Homework should be minimal but should be rigidly focused and expanded in class. Learning takes place in class and homework should be to help students gain confidence by applying their knowledge or recognizing they need help so they can gain confidence by seeing their mistakes. Ten well-designed questions that can be threaded together in class to develop a thought process will always provide better results than a hundred questions that become a chore and encourage both cheating and failure. I have seen well-meaning teachers who assigned homework every night and corrected the work once a week. Homework that isn't quickly reinforced doesn't achieve the desired effect.

Homework assigned every night becomes a burden and, as such, loses its learning potential. Homework assigned over the summer, weekend, or holiday is probably not going to be done. It is going to be copied, is going to be done sloppily, and is only going to provide any benefit to those students who are dedicated enough to learn the material regardless.

Teachers and administrators alike often point to those students who do the work and use that as a proof that homework is effective. I'm sorry folks but that 15% of the top students would achieve good grades and learn the material anyway. The fact that they did the homework is not a proof that homework teaches anything. It is only proof that the student is striving for a better grade. I have watched teacher after teacher assigned summer readings. When school starts they then develop all sorts of alternative assignments with perverse grading systems because they now need to account for those students who didn't complete their readings.

Suggestion: Let the kids enjoy their vacation then put them to work when you can guide, lead, and clarify poorly understood topics. I never gave reading assignments over economics in the summer. Why? Because even the students' parents didn't understand the concepts and all I would be doing is unscrambling misinterpreted material.

This brings us to the subject of "test reviews." This has become so prevalent that many colleges and community colleges expect professors to provide test reviews. Students are no longer required to study their text and discern what material is important and likely to be on the test. The teacher will focus their study on only the material that will be tested. I have seen test reviews that were word for word the material on the test and students still failed. One of the illuminating illustrations I used with my seniors was the case one of my graduates faced in their freshman year of college. They asked a professor for a test review and he responded he would prepare one and it would be ready the following day. The next day he arrived with copies of the textbooks table of contents and said, "When you learn what's here, you can pass my test." Now, this was a professor who understood the students' responsibility to apply themselves, and I am sure that those students began performing better in every class.

I would propose that in the junior and senior high school years all students that are taking an advanced course be required to type all assignments. They will be required to do so in college or at the work place and it is a talent that will benefit them and make their study easier and more productive. A set of notes that is typewritten is much easier to use to prepare for any exam. I can hear the response already: "Why, Mr. Ward, not every student has a computer at home." However, every school I've seen in the last 25 years has had an overabundance of computers. That same student will have to figure a way to type reports when they enter college or when preparing to submit a report for a manager at work; so let them and their parents figure out how to accomplish the task. I will guarantee if you tied it to a $100 award the assignment and/or the notes would be typewritten.

I would also propose that, in the junior and senior years, our classrooms be converted to tables and chairs. It would indicate to the students that they are about to leave the "kiddo" classroom and will allow them to place their text, notes, and assignments on the table and facilitate their work.

Being aware that much of this chapter will chafe at the sensibilities of many educational professionals, I would ask you to consider the fact that I had a <u>senior</u> ask me what a glossary was. I found it depressing when seniors turned in papers with flowers drawn on them and hearts in the corners with "I love Mr. Ward" in the margins. Are these students prepared to advance their education? Do they even understand what will be expected?

As I said before, most of our students do not fail in college because they aren't capable, they fail or drop out because they aren't emotionally prepared and lack the tools to be a student. We can't ask our teachers to be the sole responsibility for imparting knowledge to our children. Teachers cannot open their heads and scoop knowledge into them. The children must be given the tools to gain knowledge when the teacher isn't present.

For those of you who like to quote adages. This modification should sound familiar:

"Give a student a fact and you will teach him for a day, give him academic tools and he will learn throughout his life."

CHAPTER 2
Professional Incest

"Education is a kind of continuing dialogue, and a dialogue assumes, in the nature of the case, different points of view."
- Robert M Hutchins

In 1910, a study was conducted by M.L.Cooke for the Carnegie Foundation. In this "first" comprehensive study of educational management, he noted that education had two major problems. The first problem he cited was decision making by committee, which we will address later. The second was that the colleges were hiring from their own graduates. This led to a continual regurgitation of the same policies, philosophies, and paradigms with little chance of change or improvement. I would assume that we face the same issues in our lower educational levels today.

Years ago, teachers were gleaned from those who pursued a major course of study and earned a degree, which qualified them to teach. In a limited number of schools students specialized in education and teaching skills. Today, we generate a plethora of educational degrees, which are considered the "path" to becoming a teacher. The degree of elementary education is now the fad among our female graduates. If a future wife can get an elementary education degree they will be able to teach while her children are in school and have the same schedule and be available at school for the "kiddos." The fact is that if you can quote "Blooms taxonomy" verbatim, make an impressive PowerPoint presentation, and understand the Promethean Board, you are considered by many, as ready to teach.

Here is the problem: We are perpetuating the paradigm that was mentioned in the first chapter. Our colleges are teaching the elementary focus almost exclusively without recognizing the changing student needs. More critically, the schools of education have been corrupted by the academic trend of "developing" courses to justify funding. Many courses are blatantly watered down versions of rigorous academic subject matter to ensure the students don't fail because they don't meet another department's standards. This facilitates another objective; it channels funds into the college of education.

But, even if the college curriculum was modified to be more broad and inclusive another problem exists. While the public education system doesn't hire their own graduates until after they attend college, the "new" hires, through convenience sake and availability, almost always come from the same institutions with the same views and educational paradigms. Over time, this leads to a system that is adverse to change and new ideas.

Okay, so we have teachers with the same background, education, and intellectual focus - what else can that influence? Well, where do we get our administrators? Except for very large school systems that recruit out of state, we almost exclusively nurture local teachers to seek administration certification leading to a further solidifying and unbending view of educational policies that is totally resistant to change.

This leads to administrators and supervisors who are never required to gain academic training in administration and management that isn't strictly related to the college of education curriculum. I once asked an assistant superintendent if he had ever had a management or supervision course taught by the departments responsible for those classes in the college. His response was that he had taken classroom management through the college of education. This benefits the Department of Education as they gain three more hours in their discipline but, I ask you, does it provide the expertise necessary to be an administrator? Courses should be taught by the discipline that can ensure a strong foundation is studied, which then can be applied to specific educational assignments. Examples being classes in management, marketing, economics, by the Department of Business. Classes in statistics and mathematics by the mathematics department. This is not only for those who might be seeking a teaching certification in math, but for any teaching discipline to ensure they are meeting and understanding the rigor of these disciplines.

Now, what do these retiring teachers and administrators do upon retirement? They become substitutes or area consultants influencing the same systems they so enjoyed corrupting. Often, they reenter the system by attaching themselves to regional or state offices further limiting the ability to revise the system. They receive lucrative contracts to provide "continuing education" to the faculty regurgitating and re-regurgitating the same tired material.

This doesn't even begin to address the political issues. School boards are elected locally and invariably citizens believe that a former teacher or administrator is the best selection to serve on the school board. Are you following this???? We've developed a system where no one will challenge the methods and funding for the local schools. Those who should be responsible for examining the system and questioning it have been bred within the system. Does "a fox in the henhouse" sound familiar? No wonder we keep spending more and more money with less and less improvement.

As a result, our teachers continue doing what has always been done and our administrators' condone those actions because they have no background to recognize the error. Over time, the administrators learn, but the true tragedy is that many highly capable potential administrators and principles fail and are set aside because we didn't properly prepare them. Even more critical, the teachers and staff are required to endure as the same mistakes in administration are repeated year after year, as new administrators are introduced with the same tired background and must now learn on the job.

In a sincere desire to resolve these problems, we have adopted the "grocery store" method of administration. The grocery store method consists of taking untrained personnel and giving them a job as a bagger. Often, the employee shows initiative and dedication so we promote them to stocker. Then department head, then assistant manager, and eventually send them to managers' training. The problem is that they never had formal job development. To compensate, upper management directs virtually every action the managers, asst. managers, etc. make. Emails will direct daily changes to stock location and hour management along with any problem the administration is afraid the various personnel aren't capable of perceiving for themselves. This is the epitome of Micro-Management as everyone in the chain of command strives to be effective, cover their a--, and at the same time, are sincere in their desire to improve the results.

This philosophy is precisely what is pursued in education. Instead of telling an elementary, intermediate, or high school that they are an independent business unit responsible for their output, the administration invariably plays CYA (cover you're a--), principals are restricted from trying locally focused solutions. Often, personnel are hired by the local superintendent instead of by the principal. Procedures are addressed by the administration as though all three levels of education are exactly the same. This further exacerbates the "Kiddo" paradigm of "one size fits all."

So what has been the result? We have developed a system that trains our educators under a singular paradigm, hires them to a large extent in blocks, promotes them within the local system, and expects them to maintain the previously learned paradigm. In short, we have become incestuous with no new genetic input or "out of the box" development to inspire free thought and problem identification and resolution. Resulting in a continual perpetuation of stale dogma and misguided procedures.

SOLUTIONS: The solutions to this problem are not complicated but require decisive action.

First: We must make education a graduate program to be added AFTER a student has taken and shown proficiency in a major and minor taught within the requisite department and awarded the appropriate degree.

Second: Schools must be encouraged to diversify their hiring practices to recruit personnel from institutions other than the local university.

Third: Administrators must be required to earn a Master's degree and higher based on discipline courses, not "developed" educational courses. E.g.: real supervision, accounting, and management courses taught by subject professionals not "educational management" taught by generations of educators from the incestuous system.

Fourth: This is a "pie in the sky" recommendation that I hardly expect anyone to actually implement. Colleges should not allow any graduate to take an advanced education degree from that institution for a period of ten years. Students who desire a Masters degree in education should seek it at another institution. This would serve to inject various perspectives encouraging faculty discussions concerning teaching methods and program implementation.

Fifth: Professional development should require three graduate level college credits earned every year within the discipline taught or in a supporting administration discipline. (e.g.: Mathematics, English, Economics, Supervision, Accounting, Public Relations, Marketing, Speech, etc.) Today, too many schools "cookie cut" professional development through on line presentations which teachers take year after year to "earn" their development credits.

Sixth: Embark upon a program of community education encouraging the selection of school board members from outside the educational community. Elected individuals who are concerned and reasonably intelligent will quickly recognize the critical educational issues. However, these individuals might also question, "that's the way we've always done it" and "that's how education works" attitudes. Solutions may be found that were never considered because of the incestuous nature of the system.

Finally: Seek diverse administrators and develop an attitude that isn't zero sum based. An administrator can make a mistake without being a "bad administrator." Consistency is often the indication of a working system even if mistakes are made. Directing from above is detrimental to the long-range success of an organization. This perpetuates the problem of the same issues being addressed over and over instead of being resolved.

An additional problem that develops is the severe morale frustrations caused by top down direction. Think of it this way: every member of the school district works for the superintendent. Only a few work for the head of the local English department. A decision made by the superintendent will be felt by everyone. If it's good, then fine, everyone is elated. If it's a bad choice, then everyone is upset. The same decision made at the department level affects a limited number of employees and results in a more even and serene environment.

Any decision that is "passed up" the chain of command should result in the next supervisor asking why the individual at the previous level was unable to make and implement that decision. Every policy change or directive that is considered at the upper levels should be met with the question: Is this actually worth the potential ramifications or would it be better to use influence to encourage the individual managers to make and implement this concept in their own way?

Morale when decisions are made at lowest level:

Morale when decisions are made by upper levels:

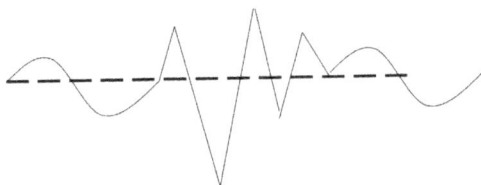

This is a good point for us to discuss the "other" problem found by Clarke in 1920. That is the use of "committees" - almost exclusively for the decision making process. A common joke among managers is that a camel is a horse developed by a committee. I used to tell my subordinate supervisors that the only effective committee consisted of three members and two were on vacation. In fact, any manager who is worth their salt is constantly embroiled in the day-to-day issues and is accumulating masses of data about their organization. Except in rare cases, no one else in the organization is as informed and able to make a decision than the manager/administrator. What can occur, however, is that decisions are delayed or satisficed. Now, satisficing has a place in the management field as an option that allows an acceptable solution without dissent. I prefer to call it a hybrid of satisfaction and comprising. It fails to deliver the optimum solution while allowing everyone to feel content. We must be careful. Committees can be morale destroyers and make incompetent managers secure.

Let's take an example. If I, as the administrator, know that we should change class starting times. I've made my decision based on months and maybe years of observation, interaction with students, teachers, and parents. Now, if I make the decision I can be sure that those who are less informed will dissent. That means I will be forced to prove my reasoning and may face some time helping everyone adjust. In the long run, this will be beneficial as the different communities recognize that I have been making decisions that were beneficial. In the short-run, and we now all think in the short-run, I will be the villain. So, we form a committee and invariably chose members from those areas I expect to face the greatest opposition. The committee takes time so that the decision is delayed. In the committee the strongest personalities sway the chosen solution. But this isn't the true problem. The problem is that we now have a situation where the decision requires no accountability. I managed to insulate myself from accountability. **IF** the committees recommended solution is successful, I can use this to show my outstanding leadership in the case of class scheduling. **IF**, on the other hand, it is unsuccessful, I can step in and demonstrate my superior decision making skills. As a result, I am shielding myself from the decision making process at the potential delay of implementation and the possibility of turmoil over a misguided option selection.

As a general rule, we should consider the two major reasons for appointing a committee. First, a committee may be used to investigate and gather facts about a problem, when not enough is known. Second, a committee may be used to present options for an administrator's consideration. These options must contain both the favorable expectations and the unfavorable. Please note that I have not said the committee would make a decision. Committee's cannot make decisions and it is imperative that administrators make that clear to the assignees.

CHAPTER 3
"LOOK-ME-UPS"
Technology and the Modern Student

"There is no lack of opportunity for learning among us. What is lacking is a respect for it...an honest respect such as we now have for technical competence or business success...We honor learning, but do not believe in it...Rather than submit to it ourselves, we hire substitutes; rather than cultivate our own brains, we pick theirs. We send as much time and energy on short-cuts to learning and imitations of learning as we do on learning itself."
- Whitney Griswold

This chapter addresses a problem that is both sensitive and controversial. That is the area of technology and education. Please understand that the author has nothing to gain by tackling this subject. In fact, these opinions have been met by a much scorn and abuse. Having said that, I still feel these are valid points that every educator and parent should consider.

Technology is, in effect, one of the primary contributors to a nation's productivity, and as such, should be lauded and encouraged. The problem is that we all fall victim to insecurity in our own knowledge and capabilities within the field. This leads us to project this onto future generations in hopes of preventing them from meeting the same shortcomings. Unfortunately, our judgment is clouded and the results are not really measuring what we wish to attain.

First: Are kids more advanced than we were? The answer: NO. They only possess a different knowledge foundation being applied to a different environment. E.g.: My father could adjust a magneto on a Model T Ford. Today most of us couldn't even start a Model T without some form of training. Yet, when I became a jet mechanic, he had little understanding of my work. He was considered extremely smart, it was not stupidity, it was simply that he wasn't current. This is very important to remember when we evaluate and plan for our students' success. Being current is not necessarily being any more capable. We can't knee jerk respond to students who are current in technology but lack the fundamental knowledge to be successful. Education must be designed to ensure knowledge is made resident in our students' arsenal of weapons. Technology is essentially a tool to assist us in implanting that knowledge. Technology is a tool that will allow a student to use the knowledge he/she has obtained in the education process. It is not capable of teaching a student or a panacea to good education. If technology were truly capable of teaching why would we have teachers????

Technology serves us, we should not serve it. This concept can change your teaching methods and the students learning habits. In many instances, we are the classic example of the "tail wagging the dog." Tremendous amounts of money and time that could be directed toward more effective learning paths are "chasing" technology as we hope for some magic solution to the degraded education system. (Much of this has been propagated by both hardware and software professionals interested is selling their products. Can anyone remember getting a computer for your school by saving box tops? Did anyone notice that that computer required proprietary software? Duh!!)

To better understand where we are going take the case of the "laptop." Most teachers today didn't own a laptop in college but all envied the student who did. It seemed to be the answer to all their problems. They would have learned so much easier and gotten so much better grades. First, there is no evidence that this is true. Second, it might be an expenditure that could have been avoided without any discernible change in learning or grade point level. The same student could have carried discs or thumb drives, each designated for a specific class. The student could hand write notes and use a powerful desktop with a large screen in the dorm to transcribed them later. This process would accomplish exactly the same effect without carrying an expensive piece of equipment back and forth. We'll address cell phones and electronic tablets later. Why then do teachers proceed to tell students they must have a laptop for college? Because they are projecting their latent desires on their students instead of rationally evaluating the situation.

In one school, I was told I had to have a Promethean interactive board so my students would learn better. Why? Because the administration got a deal on them and were looking for a magic solution to effective teaching. I tried to explain that board work allowed me all the visual assistance needed and was far less expensive. Needless to say, I got a board, put in the wrong area of the classroom. It seems it was easier to connect it if it was on the side wall. Being technologically proficient, I put it to use and as yet, we've seen no increase in student learning. Why, because a tool is a tool and they can only provide assistance, they don't teach.

The board did serve one purpose, however, it allowed the superintendent and principal to brag to the school board and public about how they had equipped every classroom with the ultimate teaching aid and were introducing technology into the classroom. Scores didn't improve within this district.

The elemental problem is one of recognizing that technology cannot teach our children. I am amused watching the progression of "on-line" texts. My personal observation is that this is not conducive to education. Teachers, who had to do it the old way by reading a text and who now have a strong grasp of the subject matter, see the on-line text as a boon where they can project it on a board and lead their students through the material. They presume that the students will go home and bring the electronic text up and study it. I'm sorry but they won't. We are teaching our students that reading a text isn't necessary and that they can "look it up." As a result, they are not learning the material in its entirety. I cannot tell you the number of students with whom I spent many hours, at both high school and college level, teaching them how to use a textbook. I once had a senior in high school ask me "What is a glossary?"

The Internet and the ability to perform research quickly is a definite asset to project development while it is a hindrance to developing an in depth understanding based on a reservoir of factual knowledge. New apps like "voice search" exacerbate the problem. It allows students to "look up" what they are interested in and avoid reading and learning all the ancillary material that knowledge is based upon. I graded papers, which were submitted with three different articles used, cut and pasted, and made no sense. This isn't the bad part; the bad part is that these students didn't have the requisite knowledge to combine the three articles into a work that made sense. They, in effect, have become a transferor of facts instead of a learning and functioning student.

Technology also has the ability to reduce learning among already capable students. The prime example I use is that of the PowerPoint or other presentation packages. Designed as a visual aid to augment the teaching process these programs are becoming the bane of good education everywhere. I will not even allow students to use these programs and force them to manually prepare presentations with visual aids. Why? Because these programs become a crutch for anyone, teachers included, where you are proud of the presentation, which you developed and begin to feel it will educate your students.

Even conscientious teachers will fall into the trap of allowing the program to teach their students. They forget that eye contact and one on one conversations yield learning. Think about the last presentation you sat through, how much did you gain? The presenter handed you a copy of the slides, after which, you stopped listening. They turned their back on you and turned down the lights so that no personal interaction took place.

One student relayed to me that the professor handed out the PowerPoint and told them the tests would be straight off the handouts. What school of teaching teaches this? Yet, it is an insidious trap into which even seasoned teachers fall. Do I use PowerPoint? Yes, but only when it is applicable and I place a blank slide between every slide so that I can address and discuss the points with my students. Remember, a hammer wasn't made to drive screws or a screwdriver to turn nuts. Technology, which isn't used properly is not an asset. Unfortunately, technology is constantly used to impress the powers to be, and convince them of a teacher's proficiency regardless of its actual effectiveness; **AND** it succeeds because so many of us are technologically challenged or woefully obsolete in its use that we assume it can now perform miracles.

You say, but what about the availability of material that technology provides? My response is that this is fantastic. I use the Internet every day and videos are wonderful assets to augment teaching, but once again, they lay a trap for the unsuspecting. We fall into the paradigm of making learning fun and easy and forget that that <u>fails to teach the student to connect facts and develop valid conclusions</u>. I would propose that prior to using these aids we ask ourselves these questions:

1. Have I developed sufficient base line knowledge for my students to apply this material?

2. Does this effectively enhance what I've taught or is it only providing a way not to teach?

3. How am I going to use this material to make my students perform at a higher level?

I learned and used technology since we had two floppy discs, one with the operating system and the other with the program we selected to use. I still remember word processors with 14" discs. I have seen the transition to the Internet and hand held devices, but most of all, I've seen us continually strive to find an "easy" way to educate. It's amazing that Socrates was able to educate anyone! He never had the benefit of computers, PowerPoint, smart phones, or tablets. He instead used what was available, as he strove to ensure his students knew the fundamentals and could express them. We need to reevaluate our use of technology and develop reasonable expectations for these tools to be a part of the answer without us assuming they are the answer. Every education class will stress "eye contact" and relationships in the learning process. Are we allowing our search for the silver bullet to abandon these basic concepts? Are we allowing our technological insecurity and generational envy to project far too much capability to our technological tools?

For those who are immediately drawn to "On-Line" courses using technology to benefit the student; I will remind you of the "Correspondence Courses" which were the perceived to be the new education salvation of the 1950's. A great deal of money was spent on these programs before we learned and accepted that only a very few individuals are disciplined enough to become educated in this manner. Yes, students will gain credits toward graduation. The question we need to ask is did they significantly improve their resident knowledge or did they only "jump through the hoops and pay their tuition".

Most importantly, are we, in fact, committing fraud? Are we using technology to avoid the hard work necessary to educate our children? Are we using technology to impress superiors? Are we convincing ourselves that we are good teachers because we are technologically proficient? And last of all are we inflating our budgets. Using technology to avoid the work and attention required to maintain textbooks and teach their use. Are we wasting financial assets on equipment and programs that won't be used or won't be used properly, so that we can impress the parents who dearly want their children to get a solid education?

CHAPTER 4
Evaluations, Progress, & Dropouts

"We lay too much stress on stick-to-it-iveness. I once had a professor who wisely hung this sign over his desk: 'Oh lord, teach me when to let go.'"
- W. G. Carleton

By now you have determined that either I am an absolute idiot or that I lack a social filter that would keep me from expressing such alienating views. In fact, there may be an element of truth in both views as I am about to illustrate.

Standardized testing has become the point of much dispute. Like any concept, it is only as beneficial as the implementation. If standardized testing becomes a political football, it cannot hope to achieve its potential. Probably the biggest problem with standardized testing is that it isn't standardized. We are constantly trying to find exceptions so that we, the educators, can justify our failures.

A standardized test can yield tremendous benefits to evaluate both our students and teachers. In order to do this, however, we must make some ground rules.

First: Test scores must not be detrimental to a teacher's retention. They will, however, be used to propose developmental training and mentoring to elevate the teacher to a level of expectations.

Second: Students should be required to perform on the tests or they will be held responsible and not the teacher. It can be expected that there will be a variability in the scores of the students, but when 70% are passing then the other 30% are at fault, not the teacher. The concept that the teacher is responsible for the test grades needs to be abandoned. The tests are traditionally given in the upper levels of education and the students must be held responsible.

I propose a system similar to the old New York Regents exams. The system allowed students to seek a "Regents" diploma or a high school diploma. One certified your readiness for college or advanced studies the other reflected an ability to persevere in a less stringent curriculum. Under this system the "Regents" diploma almost guaranteed that some college somewhere would accept your application.

Under a system similar to this, the student would be tested each year in "Regents" subjects. English, math, science, history, and foreign languages made up the core of the subjects. Other less strenuous subjects in these fields were offered in the junior and senior years. Those who passed the core subjects were eligible for graduation. Those who met the "Regents" credit hours could graduate with a "Regents" diploma.

The tests were three hours long at the end of each year. A minimum score of 65 had to be achieved. 2/3 of the test was short answer while 1/3 of the test was essay. All grading was done at the state level (similar to current AP tests). One of the major differences was that a failure was a failure. No retests were allowed and if you wanted to continue toward a "Regents" diploma or the course was a required "Regents" course, you had to retake the entire course. There were no exceptions. Students were aware of the requirement and as a result prepared themselves. We used to form study groups to prepare. We were expected to take responsibility for our failures.

Under the system four years of English and History were "Regents" standard. The first two years of Math and Science were "Regents Standard". The last two years of Math and Science were either "Regents Standard" or High School standard. Two years of foreign language were "Regents Standard" otherwise the student selected a high school elective.

The majority of students chose to seek a "Regents" diploma. However this system allowed an alternative with various business and trade mathematics and science classes that helped prepare the students to enter the work force.

But, "Won't this lead to a higher dropout rate?" I speak from experience because as an educator I am one of the few who dropped out, went into the Marine Corps, and later reentered academia. The best thing that ever happened to my high school and ultimately myself was for me to drop out. I was sucking perfectly good oxygen that other students could use. I was a disruption with no intention of conforming or ever becoming a productive student.

We tied completion rates to federal and state funding so that now we keep students that are detrimental to the process in class. The argument that kids who drop out fare worse is based on observing the true incorrigibles we now separate from the system and doesn't reflect the others who would accept their situation and go out and get a job. A real asset in addressing this problem has been removed from society's hands. We, for no explainable reason, made a high school diploma or GED a requirement to enter the armed forces. I will agree that there should be an age limit and minimum ASVAB score for entry, but generations of young men and women entered the service, earned their diplomas, and advanced to higher education while being kept off the streets and learning the discipline necessary to be successful in life.

This brings us finally to a monumental question. Why are we trying to develop nuclear scientists out of every student? I said I wouldn't try to quantify every point, but the reader can quickly research economic development as linked to math and science scores and discover that when outliers are removed, there is no significant relationship. (I recommend: "Student Achievement and National Economic Growth" by Ramirez, Luo, Schofer, & Meyer, American Journal of Education, The University of Chicago 0195-6744/2006/11301-0001$05.00)

High schools never used to teach calculus as it would be better to develop strong math foundations so that this subject could be taught in a collegiate setting. Why do we feel it is necessary today?? Why are we so focused on these subjects at the detriment of a well-balanced education? In any developed nation, there is a core of math and science professionals. These need to be replaced, and should be replaced, by a cadre of MORE highly educated individuals. If we actually want to accelerate our growth and grow our economy, we should be focusing on the 10% of exceptionally gifted math and science students and allowing the other students to pursue a solid math foundation while studying other needed skills or subjects.

A developed nation cannot expect to see increasing returns-to-scale once its core positions are filled; if it is trying to fill these positions with the same level of educational development. If a nation is growing into technology it will need a large number of scientists (the Kennedy years) but once developed it must make its gains from improving the quality of the researchers, not the number.

Unfortunately, we have been exposed and overexposed to

the paradigm that increased math and science education is going to benefit everyone. So we pay math and science teachers more, then require them to teach classes to students who are incapable of excelling in those classes. Then, wonder why there is a shortage of good math and science teachers and our students are, in remarkable numbers, forced to take a remedial math course in college. That fact alone should make it obvious that what we are doing is not working. Let's try emphasizing the fundamentals to all students and limiting the upper level concepts to the exceptional.

CHAPTER 5
Classroom Segregation

"Children today are tyrants,
They contradict their parents,
gobble their food, and tyrannize their teachers."
-Socrates

Having spoken of this topic, in passing, I feel it is necessary to examine it more closely. This is true for both teachers and parents alike. With this being mostly directed toward the administration, staff, and teachers, many of you will wonder why I would introduce the parents at this juncture. The reason is rather basic - parents are often the cause of discrimination and segregation within the system.

I am using words like segregation and discrimination for a very specific reason. These are "hot button" inflammatory terms that immediately elicit a visceral response from those reading them. This issue is one that isn't restricted to one or two specific campuses but rather is extended across the educational system.

One of the basic elements of a well-rounded education is that of socialization. When I joined the military, racial segregation was the norm in the southern states. Boot camp forced young men, from all walks of life and with every ethnic and religious background, to live together and gain a true understanding of each other. We should expect the same from our education system. Instead of having classes on diversity, our students should be experiencing diversity.

Many of you are, at this point, fuming and saying to yourselves "We don't discriminate and there is no segregation in our school." Are you that sure? Do you see entire sections of the student body that are separated because of their activities, class standing, or abilities?? If you do, then you have discrimination and segregation.

As I mentioned before, one of the easiest of these to see is that of the "Advanced Placement" classes/students. Now, some schools actually develop rigid qualifications to become one of the "Advanced" students but many become influenced by helicopter mom's who don't want to accept that their child isn't special. In either case, these students become removed from the day-to-day turmoil of the "level" classrooms. In effect, we are taking the students who will apply themselves and removing them from those who either have learning problems or are disruptive.

This has a twofold negative effect: First, it means that the children who are in the "level" classroom are influenced by students who are undisciplined and don't apply themselves. Second, the "advanced" students are in a bubble that never actually exists in real life. Learning to pick associates that are serious and forming study groups isn't necessary, as they now are joining the custom made study group of serious students.

There is a more insidious problem that this system causes. In many schools, the AP students are given special privileges. In one school I know of, the students were allowed to eat their lunch with their AP teachers under the guise of being able to ask the teacher questions. Often they were seen playing card games. If that were all that happened, it would be trivial. However, at the same time: who was at lunch? You now must try to control an entire cafeteria full of the unruly or discarded students.

The AP program lends itself to another problem. Schools take great pride in striving for AP excellence. The result is that the school often evaluates itself on two major points: How many graduates went to college and what were the results on the AP exams? It is NOT how much better the student body as a whole is performing. IF the rest of the classes are completing and passing to the next grade, then everything is fine.

Is this the only isolation of students? NO, for as long as I can remember there have been "jocks" and "nerds." These two communities separated themselves except when they had classes together or occasionally cross-dated. Today, the problem is exacerbated. Why? Because the system has established policies that facilitate segregation. Team members often are given passes that allow them to drive to and from school, miss lunch, leave a free period to go to the gym, etc. In one school, the entire band was allowed to take their lunch to the band hall so they could "bond."

I had cosmetology students ask, "Can I leave class so I can make up my hours in cosmo?" Some of these students would spend half the school day in the lab. Once again, we are developing a sub-group within the student body that is becoming isolated from the day-to-day interactions of the other students.

I witnessed agricultural students who NEVER waited for the starting bell with the rest of the student body. Why? They had a pass to go to the agricultural lab. Now, could there be a reason for one or two students to go to the lab for some form of daily maintenance. Possibly, but not for twenty or thirty to go each morning.

Are these types of policies true of all schools? Of course

not, but they are indicative of a tendency to forget that social interaction is part of developing a mature psyche. As educators and parents, we have an obligation to develop an interactive community. One where students don't form the "Us and Them" perception of their fellow students.

Some things that would help relieve some of the sectarianism would not be extremely hard to incorporate. One example would be to go back to "dress out" gym classes. Where everyone had to participate, with no exceptions. I can still remember a student nerd, who later became one of my best friends, outperforming all of the jocks in the rope climb. There was a palatable air of respect that would never have been established without that experience.

A system without "electives" until the junior year where all students must attend mandatory classes, many of which wouldn't lend themselves to AP alternatives. Let the students learn that some are good at music while others excel in art. Let the less academically gifted enjoy an opportunity to display their talents across the divides that we artificially construct.

Less drastic but far more impactful is the problem of classroom segregation. Why is this more impactful? Because it is almost universal. I have gone into classrooms that looked like a newspaper picture from the 60's. All the black students together (usually in the back), All the Hispanic students together, and all the white students together. Why? Because they chose their seats and the teacher lacked the resolve to correct the situation. I used to make them fill the next seat as they entered the room to prevent this. Now, I know, some of you will say it doesn't matter if the students are learning.

Let me relate to you a true example. I often use the military for my examples, not only because I am familiar with the military but because it is an excellent population of teenage-early twenty young adults. I ran a three story barracks for my organization and had a card file with all of the rooms assigned a card. When a young Marine checked in they were required to room in the room on the next card in order. Four men lived in each room. Many times I had personnel ask to change rooms to be with a friend and each time I refused. This meant that they had to learn to live with and cooperate with whoever was bunked with them. This was during the civil rights days and the base next to us had several racial issues. I am proud to say were not plagued with similar issues. I am convinced it is because people learned to respect each other. They would not have gained that respect if they had been allowed to isolate as "us versus them" groupings.

You may wonder why I am making such a big deal out of things that don't really hurt anyone. Well, that is the problem. In an effort to gain student allegiance/support/love/whatever, we are actually cheating them of the experiences, some of which aren't so nice, of interacting with their fellow students. It DOES hurt them over the long run, if in no other way then them not having the ability to view other students without categorizing them. What is more insidious is that we are doing these things with the belief that they are for the best. I would hope that you might consider your current policies and procedures and ways to alleviate the normal tendency for students to seek familiarity as a comfortable retreat. Is what you are doing the best policy for the entire student body's development, or is it a pacifier because we don't want to be the bad guy?

CHAPTER 6
Curriculum Structure

"If you have built castles in the air, your work need not be lost; that is where they should be.
Now put foundations under them."
-Henry David Thoreau

This brings us to one of the schools obligations subject to pressures from both academia and the general public which has slowly developed its own problems. That is the area of curriculum development. Over years the standard curriculum has been slowly altered course by course until at times it is nonsensical.

We already discussed the mathematics inequities, but these are only indicative of the overall problem. Many school systems don't offer courses that would be beneficial while others offer a plethora of insignificant and useless courses often designed to pacify the students or to deceive the parents into believing their children are receiving a "well-rounded" education.

Let's begin with the least controversial of the curriculum courses. Most people will agree that high schools need four years of English (grammar and literature including writing). Also four years of math, while the actual courses offered are open to dispute. Four years of science, again, with specific courses in dispute. Four years of History including U.S., World, Geography, and usually State. Then there is the basic requirement for two years of a foreign language. Art, music, physical fitness, speech, and technology. Most of these everyone can gather around and accept. It's the mix and match of these with "other" courses that may lead to problems. I propose that simpler is better. If we broke our high school into two tracks and simplified what we offered.

We would be much more capable of offering strong courses to prepare our students to enter the work place or academia. One track would be a college preparation track while the other would be a business and technology track. I call the second track that because it would be more acceptable to the public than to say that little Suzie or Johnny isn't mature enough to prepare for college at this time. On the other hand, Suzie and Johnny may well prefer a non-academic path in life.

Track one would consist of all four years of math, science, history, and English. Two years of a foreign language, speech, technology to concentrate on calculators (and other electronics in which we will be requiring in the classroom), as well as, their use in problem resolution, semester of art, music, and one-year physical training that can't be replaced by sports activities. Within this curriculum physical training would be a full year and would include classes in dance, etiquette, and awareness of the rules of all major sports. This would result in 22 required credits for graduation. A total of 26 credits would be required for graduation. Electives would only be allowed when a student was on track to complete the requirements.

Track two would consist of the same requirements but the math, and science requirements would be replaced with industry focused math and science applications. The foreign language requirement would be replaced with business course electives or practical shop courses.

I have inserted a curriculum example to illustrate the general approach.

	FALL SEMESTER		SPRING SEMESTER	
	College Preperation	Vocational Development	College Preparation	Vocational Developtment
Freshman	English I	English I	English I	English I
	Alegebra I	Alegebra I	Alegebra I	Alegebra I
	Geography	Geography	Geography	Geography
	Earth Science	Earth Science	Earth Science	Earth Science
	Calculators	Calculators	Computers	Computers
	Foreign Language	Shop	Foreign Language	Shop
	Phys Ed	Phys Ed	Phys Ed	Phys Ed
Sophomore	American Literature	American Literature	American Literature	American Literature
	Algebra II	Algebra II	Algebra II	Geometry
	World Hist	World Hist	World History	World History
	Biology	Biology	Biology	Biology
	Music	Music	Music	Music
	Foreign Language	Shop	Foreign Language	Shop
	Phys Ed	Phys Ed	Phys Ed	Phys Ed
Junior	World Literature	World Literature	World Literature	World Literature
	Geometry	Business Mathematics	Geometry	Finance
	American History	American History	American History	American History
	Chemestry	Agriculture	Chemestry	Husbandry
	Art	Art	Art	Art
	Foreign Language	Shop	Foreign Language	Shop
	Phys Ed	Phys Ed	Phys Ed	Phys Ed
Senior	Government	Government	Government	Government
	Calculus	Marketing	Calculus	Accounting
	Micro Economics	Intro Economics	Macro Economics	Advertising
	Physics	Botony	Physics	Selling/Sales
	Speech	Speech	Speech	Speech
	Statistics	Shop	Statistics	Shop
	Phys Ed	Phys Ed	Phys Ed	Phys Ed

Shop courses and 4 Phys Ed classes can by replaced with approved electives.

This is, of course, rudimentary and each school, district; state would need to develop their own two track system to meet their specific needs. A manufacturing area might well want courses in industrial machining while an agricultural area would rather see courses in animal husbandry.

How practical are our present offerings? What is their purpose? Does it meet the prime objective of providing Johnny with a solid foundation? No one likes to hear this but many courses we now offer are ineffective and a deterrent to the learning process and, in many cases, are expensive. The best example of this type of course, there are others, is in my opinion, cosmetology. A very expensive course that yields to young girl's imagination. If every girl taking this course became a certified cosmetologist they could not find enough heads to keep themselves busy. The course is aimed at the lower income levels and develops unrealistic expectations. In addition, students expend a large amount of effort that could be redirected.

There are programs that have proven benefits and we need to encourage and develop more of these. One school I know of has an excellent pharmacy technician program and a medical assistant program that gives high school graduates a profession with which they can earn a living while pursuing their college education. Licensed or certified programs will provide students with marketable skills and aid in retention and completion rates.

Whenever courses exist that are not developing broad based knowledge, we need to reevaluate the purpose of these courses. I often hear that they keep students interested, which reverts back to the first chapter. If we didn't offer these courses students would find interest in more germane offerings. Band, choir, theater arts are all admirable pursuits but should be extra-curricular until the junior and senior year when graduation credits can be ascertained to be on schedule and these can then be chosen as elective credits. Sports should not be a substitute for classes. Sports should be extra-curricular before or after school.

In addition to many schools using class schedule hours for sports, it results in many teachers teaching less class hours, getting a stipend, and using those hours to coach. It also results in another section of the student body being segregated from the whole. This often results in a deficit of two or more teachers to help lower class size in the core subjects. These are not radical management concepts they are business like cost/benefit considerations. It would mean that a school district would be required to stop "doing what we always do" and conduct true Public Relations with the community to unify community understanding of objectives.

There is an extension of this problem with which I was torn when considering where to place it. This subject could easily be here, with curriculum, or under funding. I decided it was a natural outgrowth of our curriculum dilemmas. This is the problem of college expense.

Today, one of the favorite issues being cheerfully adopted, as an issue, by those wanting to appear compassionate, is that of "college expense" and the burden we are placing on our young. Yet, here again we are fighting the wrong battle and will not achieve our goals. We are extending the high school curriculum failures into college. First, we now are encouraging students to seek a college education when they shouldn't. Increased demand means higher prices. Second, the majority of these students are taking majors that won't provide an annual income large enough to not place them under an unbearable burden. Let's take an example. A student pursues and attains a degree in "Environmental Studies" (Calm down it's chosen only for illustrative purposes). A noble endeavor, which leaves them $50,000 in student debt. Now Johnny enters the workforce. Low and behold, there aren't very many openings and these are met with thousands of applications each. Johnny now needs to FIND WORK. He tries the police force; no they are only hiring law enforcement degrees. He tries social work; no they only want people with sociology or psychology degrees. Finally, he gets a job in retail sales at $36,000 a year. The question: "Should Johnny have skipped college or at least chosen a different major?"

Instead of addressing the $50,000 debt we should be addressing the entire paradigm of insisting that every student should go to college. In the 50s, 60s, and into the 70s, college was an achievement and often took years of part time study to achieve. College degrees were cherished and not expected. A high school diploma was the entry pass to the work force and college graduates were the exception not the norm. Today, we act as though the college degree is the only path to success. Colleges "invent" majors to accommodate the masses trying to become "educated."

Is college debt a problem? Possibly, but we will not know for certain if we continue to consider college a necessity. What we may be facing in the long run is the penalty for misguided educational goals.

This brings us to those students who chose the right major, worked hard, and successfully completed their Baccalaureate, Masters, or Doctoral degrees. Yes, they may be facing $50,000-$150,000 college debt. But, should they be? I cannot tell you the number of high school seniors I had to sit down with and discuss their collegiate plans. Taking steps like community college for the first two years greatly reduces debt and living at home is usually the cheapest option. The problem is that many parents and even teachers consider community college a poor substitute for the "college experience" (that's academic speak for beer pong). Living at home is like sentencing the student to the "horror of horrors." Yet, both of these can impressively reduce cost. Those who attend the university away from home then must consider where to live. Dorms are usually cheaper and more convenient but then again you don't get to choose roommates and it's institutionalized. Well, what about transportation? If you live on campus there are these new inventions called bicycles, motor scooters, and busses. Most campuses are bicycle friendly and motor scooters navigate the city streets far easier than automobiles.

There is another element to college debt that no one wants to discuss - the five or six-year degree. Listen carefully, the longer you go to college the larger will be your debt. Student after student has told me they were "carrying a full load." In fact, they were taking twelve hours. They considered this a full load because it qualified them for their Pell grant. At twelve hours for two semesters, and then, of course, summer break, you will be in college for at least five years. At the same time, what is summer break? You want a degree and don't want the debt why are you not applying yourself in the summer when classes are smaller and you can cut precious time off your degree.

Now, I understand the "college experience" benefits. The question is whether or not we should even be talking about relieving college debt or if we should be educating our students and parents on the cost of the options they choose. In the 70's students wore rags, lived in dorms, ate ketchup soup, and gloried in their intellectual pursuits. Today many students believe they need to rent a condo with their friends, drive a new car, wear designer jeans, and take the summer off. Neither experience is wrong but each should leave the student with the benefits received and the debt owed.

In my Economics class I used to ask my seniors if they had had "that talk" with their parents. This often brought snickers and giggles as they had a different vision of "that talk" than I did. It was at this point, I would tell them that they were about to enter the "real world" and were old enough to sit their parents down and participate in a frank discussion about their college goals. I would advise them that their parents wanted the best for them and that as a result they might make some very poor decisions. It was for them to ensure they didn't harm their family. I would explain what their parents taking a loan on their retirement or insurance might mean and how discussing the options might help them to make decisions that were best for the entire family. I had many come to me later and say they were glad they had "that talk."

When I was younger, I once asked my father why some of the children we knew were in poverty since their great grandfather had been well known and wealthy.

"They are the victims of a sad truth, that people can expect to go from shirtsleeves to shirtsleeves in three generations," my father said.

What he meant was that a hard working laborer (in shirtsleeves) might achieve prominence and get to wear a suit and tie to work, but then his spoiled children would squander his wealth and end up with nothing. In the end, they would return to working in their shirtsleeves. We need to remember this old story when we make decisions regarding our own children's options for college.

If you continue to the end of this tome you will find I suggest a program to guide ALL parents in helping with these decisions.

CHAPTER 7
Educational Funding

"In a country well governed, poverty is something to be ashamed of. In a country badly governed, wealth is something to be ashamed of."
- Confucius

Oh boy! Al, you really want to alienate the establishment. This is often the response when this topic comes up and it is at least half true. While I don't necessarily want to alienate the powers to be, I most assuredly will. This is because I will shed light on the "not so well kept" secret - **We aren't short of money**.

Now, understand this is not to say that individual departments or individual classrooms are adequately supplied or have access to funds. It is to say that the funds are available, but most likely, they are not correctly allocated. Unfortunately, identifying the problem and the areas where this is true is made exceedingly difficult because of the psychology of budgeting. Much like the paradigm of "kiddo" education, budgeting operates under an incestuous paradigm that leads us into illogical and often counterproductive expenditures. We all have heard of the military financial boondoggles. Well, that monopoly is run by the government and so is education. The same pitfalls occur in education.

We've already seen that thousands of dollars are expended on items such as Promethean boards when conscientious evaluation might indicate that an Elmo projector, at 1/10 the price would have been sufficient and in many courses more productive. But, what causes this problem?

For you administrators, don't tell me that we are short of money "in that area." That is either a purposeful deception or an indication of a lack of knowledge and professionalism. I never worked for a government establishment that did not have a method for transferring funds across line items. It may require paperwork and a commitment to convince superiors that this is where the funds are needed, but it is possible.

First, we must take a look at the pre-established psychological mind-set we have developed, either instinctively or through ignorance. We taught all students, parents, new teachers, and administrators that there is insufficient funding for education. This lie has been perpetuated for several generations so that now it is a given. It even gives us excuses for a bad educational outcome with our children. After all, how can you blame the teachers and administration when they don't have enough money? While we expound this theory we conveniently ignore that our country has the highest expenditure of funds per student in the world and yet these other countries achieve higher test scores.

Let's go back to the incestuous nature of the beast. Educators invariably lack training in management or budgeting except what they get in limited focus courses in education. Without that training they often cannot identify misallocations or when they are identified lack the skill to address them. This is not isolated to education but is a common problem in most governmental agencies. The following is an example of how this occurs and fails to be recognized. It is a copy of an actual letter distributed to the faculty and staff:

Dear Colleagues,

This serves as your final notice that the purchasing cut off date is only 3 days away!

*The cut off for all routine purchases for the current budget year, both through the requisition process and those done through the P-Card process, will be at the end of business day on **Friday, March 28, _____**. This cut off will remain in effect for the remainder of the 2013, 2014 year. The college understands that there may be emergencies that need to be handled and those issues will be approved by this office on a documented emergency request basis only. If you have direct needs for this semester that represent priority issues for your class or work to continue then these items need to be addressed by March 28th. Just to be clear, the cut off includes the following:*

> *1.) Academic equipment and/or supplies for the remainder of the spring and summer term.*
> *2.) All faculty projects that are not already approved or of an emergency nature; this includes refresh projects and library renovations.*
> *3.) All equipment and supplies utilized by campus staff and district office personnel that are not immediate needs to continue to do business.*

Please also keep in mind that all purchase items ordered in the current fiscal year MUST BE RECEIVED IN HAND PRIOR TO JUNE 30, _____. Anything received after this date will be paid off your 2014-2015 budget.

With regard to travel in-district and in-state travel will continue as was the practice last semester, however, please review the necessity of the travel before commencing. Out of state travel will continue as per the existing process, which must be approved directly by the

*President **in advance** of any registration, transportation or reservations are made for that travel.*

Please note that purchases pertaining to grant funds and funding authorized by the Student Activity Councils on each campus will continue to be processed in a timely fashion.

Thank you for your assistance in this regard and for your patience and understanding as we work together to provide a quality education for the students of _____ County. If you have questions, please let me know.

The result of this policy is that every department rushes to spend every scintilla of their allocated funds. This often results in masses of supplies being purchased regardless of need or not. I once saw a storage shelf with over 150 boxes of paper clips and 30/50 sheet boxes of poster boards. Why? Because it would be used eventually and we couldn't give up our budget allocation. In shortsightedness no one cared that the money might well have been spent on something critically needed.

In one government agency I worked for, I was assigned to control the maintenance department and present its budget. I was told that the budget was a serious issue and we were short of funds. I was also told to add 5% to every line item and that the board wouldn't address more than four or five items so I needn't worry. I later found this to be a common approach in virtually all governmental (education) processes. Zero based budgeting is never followed, reviewed, or even understood. The result being an ever increasing bottom line.

As I began to review the individual line items I noted one for $3,600 for "dirt." For the life of me, I couldn't figure out what the "dirt" was for and no one else could tell me. I researched past years' budgets and found the line item was created six years earlier at $2,400. Investigation showed that in that year a new parking lot was built and dirt was needed for fill. The line item had been carried and increased each year and had become a "slush fund" for the administrators to shift to other areas when desired - chairs, couches, bookcases, etc. The line item had no relation to effective and efficient functioning.

I deleted this line item and no one ever noticed it was gone and the board was delighted when I proposed a budget with several of these line items deleted and the budget was lower than the previous year's.

Later, I took over the departmental supplies for one of the educational departments I was assigned and immediately provided more supplies at a lower cost and we were able to return money to the district. NO teacher in our department ever lacked for supplies, and I continually told them, if they needed something, NOT to use their own funds. In addition, we were able to provide students with supplies for projects without forcing parents to buy items such as poster board or markers.

HOW DO WE DO IT??? Well it isn't brain surgery but it does take some knowledge of budgeting and a team concept. Let me explain:

First, you must come to an agreement with your superior budgeting officer. This is essential because we often heard the saying," If we don't spend it they'll take it away." This is probably one of the most juvenile responses you can hear. If you don't spend it, you didn't need it and someone else might, so give it up...stupid. However, you and the budget superior need to make an agreement that if you turn in money to him/her you won't be penalized the following year and as a result they can expect you to always return what you don't need. This has to be an agreement between adults who understand the situation. **IF** the school board questions these departmental allocations the financial officer must defend the procedure.

Then, an agreement has to be established with the working body, faculty and staff. In the education case, the teachers knew that anything they needed, at any time (they could interrupt my classes) was available so they didn't need to stockpile supplies and I could accurately allocate the funds.

This same school later collected the "stashed" supplies from other departments and had enough supplies for a full year.

The next step is for every department and the superiors to conscientiously review each and every line item to see if we still need a line item for "typewriter repair." If not, it should be eliminated or the designation should be changed to printer repair. If so, you might find you already accounted for that line item and are going to be redundant.

For those of you who are saying, "These are problems that existed years ago or before we changed." I would like you to see if there are any questions that the following policy might engender. One school district I know of lost a bond issue and immediately placed a sports participation fee on its students. For arguments sake let's assume there were 200 student athletes participating in the various sports. Here are the questions that should be asked. First, "Is the funded budget for this year the same size, larger, or smaller than last year?" Second, "How is the (200X800) $160,000 going to be spent?" Third, "What administrative safeguards are in place to ensure the money is going to athletics?" Fourth, "Are any programs being proposed using this money that will become permanent and force budgetary considerations in the future." and Fifth, "What is the reason for this fee, is it necessary or is it a precursor to requesting a bond issue where we can tell the parents they won't face this fee if it is passed?"

This brings us to another issue with funding. When times are good we often decide we need positions that are really just a luxury. We hire more staff to do jobs that have been being done and will only provide others with more free time. The problem is that once begun these take on a life of their own and generate all sorts of functions to justify their existence until we can't easily discern what is necessary and what is not.

When in the Marine Corps, I once took over a training department and began reviewing the required reports. I sent large numbers of men to the Rifle Range each month and it was run by the Wing Training Department. I noted that one of the reports that had to be submitted each month was to the Wing Training Department on which Marine was the highest qualifier. Obviously, this was a report that was generated because someone didn't understand that they already had the information. I stopped sending in numerous reports without saying anything. No one ever noticed, until I transferred out a year later, and my replacement got concerned because he couldn't find any files on previously submitted reports. In short, work was being generated to justify positions that weren't necessary resulting in hundreds of man-hours being misallocated each month.

This same phenomenon exists in education, but even worse, it stimulates another waste in funding. Every additional worker wants the biggest and best office. In one school district, I saw six classrooms converted to office spaces. Now, you say, "Well, it might have been ok if they needed offices more than classrooms." Aside from the inanity of that statement, stop and think about the contracting expense to convert those rooms and install the requisite furniture, connections, phones, etc. Did you ever look at educational offices? The average school office makes most small business CEO's offices appear shabby. Why? Because the businessman is driven by a profit motive and won't spend their money on frivolity.

So you ask, "How do we fix it and get at the money." Well, the solution is really quite simple and the reaction will be equally as predictable. We must reduce the funding for all line items by 15%. Maintain that level of funding for two years and tell the individual business units (campuses) to find their excess and correct it. IF they claim a line item needs an increase they must quantitatively justify it. It must be done this way because otherwise they will "justify" every cut that you try to make. The enacting administrator does not normally possess the necessary hands on experience to identify the waste and has been relying on the departments to provide accurate insight. For the administrator to attempt to find the waste and fraud is impossible. E.g. Witness the federal government. Every administration says they are going to address waste and fraud and the spending keeps growing.

The reaction is predictable and you can see it on television every night. The NEA and local administrators will immediately spout gloom and doom. But a strategy of complaining about funding won't win the hearts and minds of the parents. To accomplish this, they will talk almost exclusively of the necessity to cut programs or reduce teaching staff. If their crying and moaning doesn't suffice, they will, in some cases, spitefully cut those programs and reduce staff instead of conscientiously addressing the individual line items. However, if the constraints are kept in place they will amazingly find funds, keep programs, and maintain the necessary staff. (The recent "sequester" calamity at the federal level is a fine example)

I watched administrators attend dozens of workshops, hold town meetings, hold faculty meetings, and then finally sit down to do their jobs. In one case, I saw an administrator cut the overall budget by 15% and take credit for "saving" everyone's jobs. Yet, no one questioned how this was possible. Are we unable to recognize a budget that is already out of control?

Which brings us to the elephant in the room. My own sister once posted on Facebook that it was unfair that teachers **HAVE** to buy their own supplies. I would suggest this is not only not true but is in fact part of the problem. The teaching culture has accepted this as a teachers "burden to bear." As a result, administrators consider classroom supplies a minor inconvenience for which the teachers will compensate. You notice, I did not say the money wasn't available. I once saw a school buy all new tables and equipment to equip a new conference room next to the vice principals office because it would be more convenient. The expense would have provided supplies for the entire school for a semester. In addition, we need to evaluate what supplies are actually necessary to run our classrooms. IF we want hundreds of dollars of professional posters (which teach nothing), THEN we will be required to dip into our own pockets. One innovative idea was generated by one of our teachers to make available pencils for the students when they forgot one. We bought golfing pencils. The students weren't deprived but no one wanted to take them home. Our expense for pencils dropped significantly. Any time a new program is begun, a piece of furniture is bought, or a beautification project is undertaken, we need to ask ourselves if the basic classroom supply needs are being met. If not, then we need to do some serious soul searching.

For those of you who are screaming about the compensation teachers receive, I would remind you all situations are different. In many cases an argument over workload is more appropriate than one over pay. In some cases a honest look at procedures will help. (Turn back to the discussion of homework.)

However, there is a dirty little devil in the room that takes advantage of our teaching professionals. Whenever a bond issue doesn't pass or in the period leading up to the bond issue, school boards love to moan over the lack of funds to compensate teaching staff. In many cases, there is a shortage of funds. In other cases, it is exactly what it appears. This in itself would be bad enough but then the real deception begins. In order to retain the staff and faculty and appear generous, the school board approves a bonus for all the workers. It may be across the board or it may consist of a complicated formula so everyone feels it is fair. Here's the twist: NO BONUS MONEY is applied toward retirement. I have known school districts that didn't enact a pay raise for ten years and relied upon the bonus system to retain personnel. Unfortunately, many of our younger education professionals aren't looking far enough down the road to put an end to this practice. I will remind you that administrators, at all levels, are more often concerned with the appearance of being productive and that pay raises never appear to be reflective of their ingenuity and diligence.

This chapter could go on for hundreds of pages but then I would be teaching management not trying to posit ideas for consideration. The important point is to recognize that education in total is not underfunded (some departments may be due to misallocation). It suffers from the inherent poor management seen in most governmental agencies. It uses the citizens concern for their children as a tool to achieve goals that bear no relationship to producing a superior product. In short, it is an inherently inefficient system administrated by poorly trained management.

NOTE: I DID NOT say management was ill intentioned.

CHAPTER 8
Parents, Communities, & Public Relations

"Could I climb to the highest place in Athens, I would lift my voice and proclaim, "Fellow citizens, why do you turn and scrape every stone to gather wealth and take so little care of your children to whom one day you must relinquish it all?"
- Socrates

One area that is the hardest to understand is that of public relations. In a profession that must constantly deal with large groups of individuals (students) from a variety of backgrounds, we are sorely lacking in the skills to facilitate both our efforts and those of the profession in general.

If we accept, as a given, that parents honestly want their children to get a valuable education and that educators want to contribute to society by providing that education, then why do surveys show that teachers view the parents as one of the major obstacles and parents view teachers as inadequate?

The answer is simple, while we emphasize relationships within the classroom and ask teachers to contact parents; we do virtually nothing to actively promote the relationships necessary to successfully develop a synergy between the community and school district. As a result, some teachers develop a working relationship with the parents, on their own, while others do not. This results in a disjointed public opinion of education based upon individual teachers and a time and case specific attitude. If Johnny happens to have Ms.

Schmucktella, then the system is wonderful; if he has Mr. Grouch, then it's terrible. If a new policy is established, it may or may not be discussed with the community and the resulting reaction can almost be predicted. Yet, although predictable, we fail to take the steps to avert the avalanche of parental discourse.

Invariably, successful schools establish a working relationship with their community. This doesn't mean a PTA made of the "elite" mothers and teachers. It means a true working relationship where parents, teachers, and administrators actively discuss issues and pending events.

I cannot tell you how many times I have heard from various teachers, from a number of different districts, that "our community" wouldn't approve of that type of action. How do you know? Without interaction and discussion, you are assuming that your biased view of the community is globally accurate.

There are any number of actions that can be taken to remedy this problem but one of them must revert back to the issue of incestousness (word coined by me). If we promote from within and elevate a teacher to the public relations position within our district, then we are placing a person into a position that is community sensitive who has already formed opinions about the community. We all shudder at the term "profiling" but this type of assignment is "profiling" an entire community. With the amount of money expended within a school district it is not absurd to expect a professional public relations department, staffed with at least an externally recruited individual.

Next, make public relations a daily objective. All administrators should make it a rule to daily contact someone in the community, that is not a parent dreading the call, and discuss the school and find out their opinions. Don't use these periods to focus on the negatives, but to learn what the perceptions are in the public of the districts efforts.

We must be careful not to allow the "bloom on the rose" to distract us. Yes, there are a number of sincerely enthusiastic parents and community members. Yes, they work their hearts out; but they are not the community. It is very easy to work with them and pat each other on the back believing we are enacting policies approved of by all. As true as it is that we have students that will always be successful there are also community members who will always support us. Our objective should be to reach out to the rest of the community.

I have seen districts where "open house" was a three-hour affair for parents to "drop by." So, who shows up? The parents who care about their child's education. They aren't the problem but they are the only ones we address. What's wrong with a full day with parents allowed to ride busses bringing their children to school? Displays to show what the school is achieving: PowerPoints in every room to illustrate the activities the teacher is using to engage the students, discussion sessions addressing various subjects - All organized professionally with agendas and campus maps for all attendees.

Why can't the school participate in every community activity? A number of floats in every parade, speakers in local radio talk shows, volunteers at the local library, volunteers at blood drives, and any other community activity, well coordinated and with a centrally aimed goal.

In the days of "Harvard Graphics", a graphics package similar to PowerPoint, I was in a position to convince my university of a program to gain community support. We went to the local mall and got permission from the mall to use several of their display windows to mount computers with a looped program. Each month a different discipline would put on a continually running slide show with various physical artifacts surrounding the computer. E.g. a skull and bones for archeology. It cost us nothing, but we received a great deal of input and gained from the community awareness.

Ok, so I'll say it. There are different communities with different cultures within every district. We make every effort not to consider this, as we now want to be a generic society. Well, that is not only unrealistic but also detrimental to achieving our goals. So, why not make every effort to get each of our various communities to recognize the districts issues and assist in finding remedies. We can't say that one community cares more about their child's education. If we do, we are the guilty parties.

Why not, contact the various influential members of each community and schedule seminars and meetings. Why not use the local civic group meetings as learning sessions for the community? When I was a military recruiter, I used these sources and, as a result, I was welcomed into campuses that had always excluded recruiters. It was, most often, a matter of communicating and building trust.

Why not call parents and ask them to help with the prom, open house, ball game refreshments, etc.? I learned a big lesson as master of my lodge. When I asked people to help, they developed a sense of ownership and soon were volunteering. Even when they declined, they later would contact me to see "if there was anything else they could do." Don't rely on organizations to manage these events, where it will become a select few participating.

One area I often hear discussed is the Latino community

and the lack of language skills. Why not get some of the Latino leaders to get various Spanish speaking families to help with the concessions at the soccer games? They will recognize the game, feel needed, and interact with the rest of the community. Ask for Latino volunteers to address the Spanish classes in their language and dialect. These are but a few ideas but the effort has to be made.

Why not develop a policy where every teacher in every discipline must prepare a 30-minute presentation to be given to the public, and develop a speaker's bureau with the local business organizations, governmental agencies, and churches. The public would witness educators' proficiency, while the teachers would gain a sense of the communities concerns. Oh! If public relations doesn't seem important to some use this as a justification for your new technology initiatives.

CHAPTER 9
Culture, Teachers, Students

"In one McGuffey's Reader there is a story about the clock that had been running for a long, long time on the mantelpiece. One day the lock began to think about how many times during the year ahead it would have to tick. It counted up the seconds - 31,536,000 in the year - and the old clock just got too tired and said, "I can't do it!" and stopped right there. When somebody reminded the clock that it did not have to tick the 31,536,000 seconds all at one time, but rather one by one, it began to run again and everything was all right."

- Nenien C. McPherson, Jr.

This chapter addresses and readdresses many of the subjects formerly discussed. While somewhat redundant, it is necessary because we forget that the cultures we live and work within are made up of many of the attitudes and experiences in which we are entrapped.

First, we need to examine the culture that exists within the classroom, school, district, and system. It quickly becomes obvious that high achievement and low achievement schools have very little difference in student mental capabilities. If this is true, then why is there such disparity in student achievement? The stock answers are that either we hired poor educators or that we have a community culture that supports failure. Both are, of course, wrong but more importantly they are at the very least excuses for poor management and misdirected efforts.

I once had a principal tell me, "You can't teach the way you are because not every student will be entering college." To me, this was a red flag, as I had dropped out of high school and later gone back. I asked the principal to step into the hall and then asked, "Point out the student who isn't going to ever go to college." To me this is an indication of a culture within the school, and possibly the district, that accepts less than optimum achievement by the students and is in fact profiling an entire community.

We also must to be careful that we don't attempt to incorporate policies, programs, or technology based on the fact that we see it working somewhere else. Is our culture mature enough to accept this idea? Do we have the facilities, knowledge, maturity, or physical assets to make this idea effective and financially efficient?

A good example of the right idea going wrong can be seen by examining JIT inventory management. In the 90s, note was taken that the Japanese had a program that demanded supplies for production were delivered at an extremely rigid time schedule. This meant that supplies were available exactly when needed and funds weren't committed to maintaining inventories of supplies to be used later.

The problem was that no one recognized this is no more than an extension of good management. If the management in control knows their capabilities, they will, inherently, attempt to reduce inventories and allocated funds. Where Japan was a small island with an internalized supply chain, the U.S. is comparably huge and its supply chain has been broadly spread as the country has developed. As a result, while the IDEA of JIT is valid the capability to implement will vary by individual delivery potential.

Because many companies tried to "force" JIT to meet Japanese expectations JIT failed in most cases and earned itself a bad name for most managers. In reality, the concept should be pursued but it should be pursued according to the capabilities of the individual industries supply chain.

Education units need to recognize and accept that good concepts may not be adaptable or may only be able to be partially adaptable within their culture. The efforts should be to determine what is realistically possible. Within education PLC is an excellent example of a program that is right on target.

The problem is that, much like JIT, it isn't universally applicable. Those districts with mature leadership have either already incorporated the concepts or are fertile ground to adapt portions of it. Those who aren't blessed with that level of managerial maturity will not be able to perform the program at the same level.

Successful schools regularly exhibit a culture that is conducive to student learning. Teachers are continually seeking to improve the learning process, while students are actively participating and seeking knowledge. But, we cannot be too careful ensuring that we don't get caught in a self-defeating course of perpetual failure.

I guess the best illustration is one I used with a principal. I once asked this principal if they would release a brand new puppy onto the living room carpet before it was potty-trained or would potty-train it first. This is important because we can introduce all sorts of "open learning" innovations that we see work in other settings without properly preparing our teachers, administrators, and students.

If we do this we will suffer failure and then will discard

the idea, and poison the well, without it ever being given the proper venue. As a result, we will never gain the benefits that the other campuses received from the implementation of whatever procedure it was.

Now, to nurture a cultural environment that can take advantage of the "best practices" we observe in other schools or districts we must begin a program of self reflection and analysis. It will only be when we know our own cultural mores and limitations that we can make the changes necessary to accept the more innovative and practical methodology used by the more successful campuses.

First: Every administrator who professes a desire to improve must accept that the quality of education is their mission. It is not to impress the "Board" or to be liked by their staff. It is not to be the "cool" principal that the students love. It is not to be recognized for the "big programs/policies put in place. Many of these things are to be desired but without significant change in the students' achievements, are a sign of a system of administrators that are caught in the whirlpool of self-gratification and nepotistic backslapping.

Second, and maybe the most important: Teachers must accept that their function is to "develop" academically oriented young men and women. We must abandon the concept that it is our job to teach and 'impart knowledge." We must work as a synergistically growing and maturing team. All too often, viable and progressive ideas fall by the wayside because the actors most responsible for the implementation are the most poorly trained and fail to understand their responsibilities in ensuring the program is successful. This is a systemic problem that is made worse by the incestuous nature of educations personal makeup as described in Chapter 2. Teachers who need the requisite counseling and training fail to receive it because of the inability of the administrators to recognize the need, or for their unwillingness to alienate lifelong friends and colleagues.

Third: The students must be weaned of the paradigms that direct them to expect specific unhealthy practices and instead should become expectant of vibrant and productive change within the system. This must, however, be change within a framework of consistency. New programs or procedures must be presented to the students well ahead of implementation with thorough explanations of the goals and expected results. Each student must recognize their responsibilities as they begin to adapt and interact within the new procedural methodology. This is especially critical when it is a fundamental change in teaching methods, curriculum requirements, and/or testing procedures. I once saw a school attempt to make a major grading change after the Christmas holidays. Why would anyone inject this type of turmoil into the middle of a school year? They failed to recognize the need for both student and teacher preparation!

Fourth: We have to continually ask ourselves: If the proposed changes are designed to improve education or only to entertain the students or impress the school board or parents. No efforts should be made that affect the teaching day, methods, or curriculum without a sound indication that it will significantly improve the process of education. A change that is made for appearances sake whether to gain parental approval or impress the School Board should not be undertaken. While not as glamorous, the day-to-day business of educating students will, over time, yield far more impressive results at a much reduced cost.

CHAPTER 10
Program Management
(The Peter Principle on Steroids)

"The tumult and the shouting dies; the captains and the kings depart: still stands thine ancient sacrifice, an humble and contrite heart. Lord God of hosts, be with us yet, Lest we forget- Lest we forget!"
- Rudyard Kipling

A serious trap we can fall into is that of becoming "program managers." I knew administrators, both in education and business, who made a career of "implementing programs." Most of which, didn't work and left a poisoned well legacy behind them. The implementer receives accolades for the program when it is implemented and no penalty when it fades into oblivion. Accepting position after position, he/she progresses up the ladder leaving behind a true legacy of misspent funds, wasted man-hours, and diversion from accomplishing our true mission, the education of our youth.

You notice, at no time did I say that these innovative programs are not good ideas. Au contraire, they are usually extremely progressive. The problem is that they are "cookie cutter" ideas that haven't been modified to fit the situation and more importantly the academic culture has not been adequately prepared to embrace the concept. Now, this does not mean staff development classes to affect a "buy in." A term that is always used by educators, who don't understand the basic management concept of a "buy in."

What I am referring to is a cohesive effort to examine, modify, and implement the idea while informing all concerned parties of the goals and objectives it is intended to achieve. This must reflect an educational improvement objective or the entire concept is wasting valuable time and resources, regardless of how much it is "liked, enjoyable, or fun."

Educators tend to be isolationists, partly due to our individual methods and partly due to a misunderstanding of "academic freedom." This tendency must be fought at every level because it becomes fodder for the "program manager." Instead of working as a team to improve the education throughout the system, we find personal pride in our individual efforts. This means that any program intended to be universally applicable is doomed to failure. No matter how progressive or valuable, it cannot succeed without teamwork. Not teamwork in one or two seminar sessions but teamwork applied day after day across departmental lines.

A fine example of this was witnessed when a school district incorporated the previously mentioned PLC program. The program was well designed and undoubtedly benefited many districts throughout the country. The problem was that while it drew accolades for the administration it was an expensive venture and wasn't embraced universally. It also lacked administrators who understood the amount of time and revision the program would require to fit the district. As a result, one year later I spoke to several teachers who said PLC was working fine in their department while other departments were cursing the entire venture. In both cases the program had failed. The program was designed to be a campus wide effort and while individual departments were utilizing some of the concepts the intent of the program was being ignored.

Now, you might say it would have worked if everyone had "bought in" to the idea. Wrong - most of the faculty looked forward to the expected results. The problem was it had not been properly staffed, implemented, and the personnel did not comprehend the need for intra-departmental participation and cooperation.

It was discontinued in the district, but not until many consultants got paid, thousands of teacher man-hours were expended, and the School Board was impressed with the **efforts** the administration was making. You notice I say efforts not accomplishments. As a result the individual who championed the program gained from the notoriety and departed as the program failed, to a far more lucrative position.

I suffered through schedule changes, clothing regulation changes, lunch hour changes, tutoring changes, technology changes, etc. Each time the following question should have been asked, "Are we doing this to improve the education of the student or are there other motives?" I propose we most often make changes on big issue items to accomplish one of the following goals:

A. Impress the School Board
B. Impress the Superintendent
C. Impress the Parents
D. Hide the fact that we are either incompetent or so overwhelmed we must divert attention.
E. Are worried that "the doing of the day-to-day ugly grunt work" won't leave the appearance we are doing our best.
F. We are deluding ourselves into believing other people

are "better" or "more capable" of running our campus than we are.

So, how do we stop "program management" and ensure only constructive and effective steps are being taken to improve our students education.

First: Ask ourselves the same old question: "Is this intended to significantly improve age old educational techniques and/or methodology or is it only to meet one of the previously listed objectives?"

Second: Address the day-to-day operations with attention to detail so programs with merit can be quickly identified and their appropriateness for application in our situation is evident.

Third: Begin a program of cross-departmental communication and cooperation in order to make any universal implementation more easily undertaken.

Fourth: Gain an understanding within ourselves and with our staff so everyone understands how many changes are administrative prerogative and loyal employees don't need a "buy in" for <u>every</u> change. Ensure major policy or procedural changes are thoroughly vetted and discussed prior to a final decision and the responsibilities and expected actions of all players are clearly defined.

Fifth: Begin a policy of immediately examining the day-to-day productivity and attention to detail of any manager who proposes sweeping change without proper staffing.

Sixth: Examine whether a "program" is needed or a change in management is appropriate. By this I do not mean, necessarily, the boss. Look closely at the players, especially those having been in place for a long period, and ask yourself if this program would even be a discussion if they were all operating as a team and gaining from the natural synergy which is present in any educational environment.

Program management is an insidious devourer of resources and effort. It detracts from the hard day-to-day drudgery necessary to be successful in the long run. It encourages promotion reminiscent of the "Peter Principle," and discourages hard working and conscientious employees. I propose all school districts could be successful and provide a far better education if we would stop attempting to find the "Silver Bullet."

Unfortunately, school boards and administrators will face a difficult fight. In the 80s and 90s, America embraced a philosophy of "up or out." This meant your career was viewed as a failure if you didn't show accomplishment or promotion. Prior to this, many front line managers would be in place for ten years or more without promotion. This led to careful consideration of implemented policies because the people doing the implementation had to live with the results. Today, new teachers or administrators EXPECT to see a raise, promotion, accolade, or some other illustration of their value on a regular basis. This has led to a literal cesspool of consultants, programs, technological innovations, etc. Not all bad but not all appropriate for each situation and the decision will have to be made knowing someone, maybe a superior, has staked their vested interest on the proposition.

The term "Vested Interest" should be burned deeply into every administrator's gray matter. Any program, policy, or procedure incorporated has been championed by someone. Whenever, a proposal is made to change policy/procedures or implement programs a quick analysis must be made of who has a vested interest in not making the change or has earned their reputation based upon the old policy, program, or regulation. This includes a self-examination to determine whether or not you are willing to abandon your own security blanket. If either you, or others you can identify, feel a vested interest then a "buy in" will be essential to any change. But buy-in is only applicable to those individuals. The others will readily make any change with minimum explanation.

CHAPTER 11
Why?

*"The true teacher defends his pupils
against his own personal influence."*
- Amos Alcott

I saved this chapter until the end. Why? Because I wanted to ensure there was a perspective lent to the final set of suggestions. Many of my friends asked me why I am even trying to write this, as in their words, no one will pay attention.

In order to explain why, it becomes necessary to view education from the perspective of a failure. You see, as a student I was a failure. I failed high school and quit. I failed at electronics school in the Marine Corps and got reassigned as a jet mechanic. I saw education as something I couldn't conquer, until I wanted to reenlist in the Corps. I was told I had to get a GED (fairly new then) and to go down and take the test. I was frightened to death. I took the test with no preparation and passed on the first try. They asked me if I wanted to take the two-year CLEP. (In those days you could get two years' college credit) I said, "Why not?" I passed on the first try.

Suddenly, I realized that **I** wasn't the failure. I began to scrutinize every training lecture and school I was sent to and found that almost universally the failures were in the expectations and presentations. These two entities weren't being synchronized to deliver the greatest outcome. Presentations were being delivered as though the students were incapable of rational thinking and the expectations were that they would only absorb a minuscule amount of the material.

Later, while in the USMC, I wanted to get my A.A. degree. The college on base was only offering a Master's Degree program. I asked if I could apply these courses toward my A.A. Being told yes I took my first college class, it was ancient literature and my first assignment was to present a 20-page comparative analysis of the Odyssey and the Iliad. I immediately learned that I had been programmed to expect too much of my teachers/instructors/professors. It was **my** responsibility to learn the material and, also, to force them to earn their salary by explaining what I didn't understand.

I taught for the Marine Corps at various times. I was an instructor at jet mechanics school in Millington, Tennessee and taught, then ran, the career planning school for the Western Pacific in Okinawa. After retiring, I elected to pursue my B.B.A. and M.B.A., later making an attempt at a D.B.A. In that case, family issues caused me to drop the program but later I pursued additional graduate courses to facilitate teaching. I became a community college instructor and later, a department head, then retired to be near my daughter. There, I began teaching at the high school level, eventually retiring. All of this is in the section "About the Author." What isn't in that section is the fact that I formed some very strong feelings about our educational system. These include a true heartfelt agony over the efforts many dedicated individuals are expending, often in pursuit of the wrong objectives. Also, a belief that reflection and self-analysis can lead us to improving the outcome we all so desperately want for our students.

I know and understand the wonderful feeling of being the "Mr. Chips" of education. Each of us wishes we could be the greatest influence on each of our students and earn the respect and adoration we feel our hard work deserves. The problem is that being an educator, at any level, isn't a glamorous career. It is a day-to-day, dog eat dog, which leaves others unthankful of our combat. Yes, it has something in common with combat. It consists of hour after hour, and day after day, of drudgery followed by a brief interruption of sheer terror or adulation.

That is hard to accept so all of us, myself included, often get sidetracked into chasing the rabbit trail, which might lead to glory. We make "super" presentations, spend money on classroom decorations, and dedicate time trying to save every wounded student, time that we could be using to improve all of them. These things are usually done so we can feel that sense of accomplishment. The problem is that we are spending time and money pursuing the shadow of our objective. This is aggravated, even more, by a system that consists of administrators who are just as frustrated. Because education isn't glamorous, they must also dream up radical solutions to impress the school board and convince the public they are effective. Once again, not addressing the goal of IMPROVING our students' education.

What I would hope is that the perspective of a failure might cause each of you to take a different view of the entire educational system. Not from a view of disapproval, but rather, with a critical mind's eye examining it for false pathways. As easily as the hound can course down a rabbit trail, instead of pursuing the original prey, we can also be deluded into thinking we are doing the right thing.

In the next section, I will be suggesting some potential

solutions for consideration. I then have left blank lines for you to take notes and propose solutions to the problems you see in your own system. Administrators, please encourage parents and teachers alike, to comment so you can see if any of the problems suggested exist within your own district.

Why? Because as I grow older, I still hope to make a difference.

CHAPTER 12
Summary and Suggestions

"A widely prevalent notion today seems to demand instant achievement of goals, without any of the wearying, frustrating preparation that is indispensable to any task. As the exemplar of a way of life, the professional-that man or woman who invests every new task or duty, no matter how small, with discipline of mind and spirit-is a vanishing American, particularly among those who too often believe that dreams come true because they ought to and not because they are caused to materialize."
- Jack Valenti

Within all the Negativity of this work is hidden an important element, which gives us hope, and is necessary if we are to revitalize our educational system. **This element is the unselfish and dedicated efforts of the greatest majority of our hard working educational professionals**.

If this work has done nothing else, I hope it has encouraged everyone to examine their own situation and address the areas needing attention. We have all heard the saying, "A mind is a terrible thing to waste." Well, if we are placing dedicated people into classrooms operating under false paradigms and "vested interest" policies and procedures, then we are effectively wasting valuable minds in a futile effort to improve an outcome using the wrong tools.

In my dreams, I visualize school staff development seminars addressing the issues outlined in this work. In that dream, open discussions ensue which lead to correcting those issues that apply to that specific district. Where these issues aren't apparent the discussions generate numerous other problems that haven't been addressed. Instead of paying thousands of dollars for an outsider to tell your teachers/staff that they must adjust their blue-pink-or lavender personality, you will actually be solving problems.

The following is an accumulation of ideas I hope might help any district to excel. Some of the ideas are simplistic in nature while others would require considerable effort and even cross discipline and intra-school development. I am not suggesting these as "cure all's" but hope to stimulate others to approach our educational problems with a questioning attitude.

First: is more a concept than an actual plan. This was developed when I was a maintenance chief in the Marine Corps. The basic tenet is one where ALL organizations strive to be continuously improving. During this time, and currently, most people interpreted this as incorporating a sweeping and organizational changing program. I could not see a reason to be so invasive; instead I introduced the **3 and 1** initiative. Now, understand the times and numbers are subjective and should be designed to fit your school or district.

It worked like this: All department heads had to submit, in the departmental meeting, three minor changes they had incorporated each week. It is extremely important not to belittle any effort and allow any department to incorporate an idea another department may have used the previous week. With 16 departments this had the potential to generate over 800 minor improvements in any given year. These "small" changes could be as easy as putting liners in the trashcans, repainting the safety zones, putting a paper cup dispenser next to the water fountain, etc. Over time the departments improved their projects as they saw the effect.

The number one stood for a major recommendation. Each department was required, once a month, to propose a major improvement, which had the potential to benefit the department or the entire unit. Many of these would be "trial balloons" having little chance of accomplishment but would help focus attention to various needs and potential solutions.

Did it work? Yes, in fact, the biggest problem became thinking of a minor project that hadn't been done. When we faced an Inspector General's inspection the Commanding Officer asked me what steps or inspections I had to take to prepare, I gleefully said NONE. This does work, and departmental meetings get to be fun as the department heads joke about the various projects.

Second: Begin a policy of cross-discipline assignments and grades. Ask teachers to align assignments so that a students paper for history may also be submitted for their English assignment. Allow students to earn a grade for the History research and a grade for the English grammar and developmental writing. This would reduce that student's workload while improving their ability to do research and formulate it into an acceptable written work.

Third: This is an idea I developed when teaching High School History, Government, and Economics. It was never followed up on, as I wasn't in the position to get participants. This would be an exceptional aide to education at all levels. Here is the concept:

Make a timeline identifying ten/fifteen/twenty critical dates of human development.

An example which is designed for illustrative purposes is presented here these dates were only selected as examples:

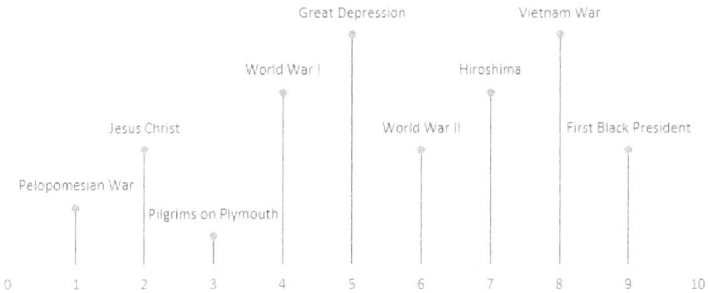

Require each discipline identify the transitional events within their discipline and insert these into the timeline keeping the baseline dates in place. Position the base time line in each classroom in elementary school.

Below, is an illustrative example of a time line for an art class, with three dates entered. Again, these dates were only selected as examples and it is obvious I am not an "art" major.

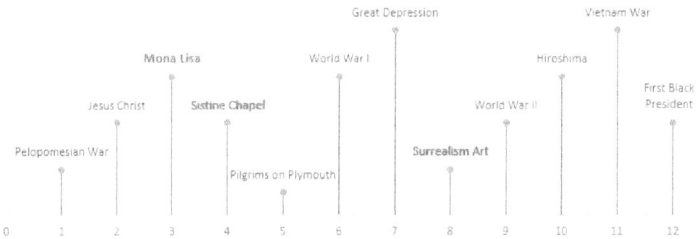

Position the departmental timelines in the classrooms where the subject material is taught in each class through high school.

What is the advantage??? Students, from grade one on, would identify the baseline dates and easily associate them with the dates for the subject studied. Students would realize Shakespeare didn't live in the 1900's and Alexander the Great wasn't in WWI.

Fourth: Perform a regular examination of staff and faculty resumes and experiences. This may seem simple but it is a mainstay of good managers. All too often administrators and even fellow faculty have no idea of the competence surrounding them. They are so busy meeting the day-to-day issues that they fail to perform this simple act. In one school where I worked I know we had a NASA engineer, a retired company CEO, and a previous Public Relations officer. Yet the administration would bring in consultants and trainers who were far less qualified to address many subjects than these individuals. Using them to provide staff development would be less expensive, would bolster staff respect for each other, and might inject totally new perspectives. Additionally, it may provide resources for all types of issue resolution and possibly replacements for staffing considerations.

Fifth: Institute a policy where all School Board Members, Administrators, Principals, Asst. Principals, and Department Heads would be required to take a comprehensive course in zero based, line item accounting/budgeting.

Sixth: Select and develop teachers and staff to form a "speaker's bureau" to present to the public the schools efforts and discuss the school/community relations. Presentations could focus on specific departments and how they functioned within the system and could enlighten the public to the schools efforts. Church's, fraternal organizations, charitable organizations would be the focus and a goal of three presentations each month could be the standard. Ensuring throughout the year the dialogue is consistent and no one presenter is overburdened.

Seventh: This will cause a revolt. Require principals to conduct a formal weekly inspection of their campus accompanied by different department heads each time. There is no better way to be aware of what is being overlooked and department heads gain by ensuring their areas of responsibility are not disregarded. For those who say, "When are we going to find time?" I would respond: a set time e.g. Friday morning, is better than having something go terribly wrong or the amount of time you will devote to "fixing" a long standing problem.

Eighth: I witnessed an exceptional AP teacher leave a campus and take some of the best designed lesson plans and Promethean Board presentations with him because, "I developed them and if you want this develop it yourselves." This individual was not bitter. He had developed a distorted view of "Academic freedom" I propose departments keep a file of "exceptional" lesson plans and presentations to ensure continuity across classrooms. Most teachers will modify these or develop their own but in cases where a substitute is needed or there is a question of continuity these can be invaluable. In addition, we are all learning animals and new teachers often stumble as they search for the "best way" to deliver a lesson. These can provide any new teacher with a blue print and ideas for him/her to develop their own style.

At this point you will notice not one item has been addressed to improve individual student learning. There is a reason. IF the system improves its efficiency it will be easier for the individual teacher to address the basic goal of student learning.

Ninth: REQUIRE out loud reading in class at the elementary and intermediate level. A student cannot tell if he/she is pronouncing correctly or even saying the right words with the proper emphasis unless someone is correcting. It also helps other students to identify common errors.

Tenth: ALL students should be required to recite their "times tables" **out loud** in elementary school and should have an oral test on them. Far too many activities demand a working knowledge of the multiplication process, from long division to factoring equations to making change (this is one of the few memorization drills I whole-heartedly believe we need our students to do. I had seniors who couldn't tell me what 7X8 was and when I queried them they said, "Why learn them when I have a calculator?").

Eleventh: as mentioned previously, require all students to keep comprehensive notes in every class. (Notes not Journals. A Journal is a diary and in school we take notes) Develop a specific format and a rubric for grading these notes.

Twelfth: Establish school wide standards for assignments. APA OR MLA, heading, margins, font, double/single spacing, paper color/quality, cover page or not, folder or not, penalty for late submission. Come on folks you are going to send them to College-get them prepared.

Examples might be:

1. All work will be submitted in APA format.

2. Paper margins are expected to be 1"x1"

3. All work will be double-spaced.

4. Paper is expected to be standard white

5. Submitted papers will contain a "cover page"

6. All works typewritten or handwritten will use a uniform heading: an example being......

Name
Date
Class
Assignment
Teacher

7. All pages will be numbered, center/bottom.

8. Works will be stapled in upper left corner.

Now understand, different schools, districts, etc. will establish their own preferences but students need to learn conformity is not an evil plot by adults to diminish their talents. Students who learn to color within the lines inevitably produce better results.

Thirteenth: In the military, Millington Aviation Training, we had a testing center. At the beginning of the year all the instructors submitted questions on their discipline to be added to the test bank. When a teacher needed a test he requested it from the testing center with no input, administered it, returned it, and got the grades with notations on any question reflecting, statistically, to be faulty over time. This made testing more uniform and quickly alerted teachers to areas being overlooked or poorly taught.

With today's electronics there is no reason a similar system couldn't exist within our districts. I always grinned when teachers talked about "benchmark" exams but each teacher gave their own. A benchmark should extend across classrooms and teachers. Having a central generation source will allow a true comparison and will prevent complacency as teachers tend to teach in the areas they are most familiar.

Speaking of "Benchmarks" we need to ensure teachers and administration fully understand the purpose and use of these excellent tools. A Benchmark **IS NOT** a reflection of the teacher; it is a signal of the class's level of understanding and a highlight of areas needing attention. A Benchmark **SHOULD NOT** be a one-time test, entered into the files to meet a requirement, and then forgotten. It should **ALWAYS** be re-administered without the same questions but with well selected, similar questions, to reflect the classes growing competency.

Fourteenth: All High School classes should contain an element of College preparedness, or vocational goals, built into the class and High Schools should have regularly scheduled workshops for parents and children alike. Now, by preparedness I am not discussing academic preparedness. Rather, I'm talking about life affecting decisions related to college. Parents and Students should be discussing subjects such as college choices, living options, course loads, etc. so when students choose college they don't place themselves in a burdensome situation.

YOUR ideas, unique to your school:

_____

_____

_____

_____

_____

_____

_____

_____

_____

_____

_____

_____

_____

_____

_____

_____

_____

_____

_____

_____

ACKNOWLEDGEMENT

"Real friends are those who, when you've made a fool of yourself,
don't feel you've done a permanent job."
- Confucius

I would be remiss if I didn't acknowledge who helped me in this work.

Alexys Akey has provided editorial help, but even more significantly, she has leant the insight of a former student to my musings. I am listing Alexys as a contributor; as without her efforts, this work would have been more tedious and less likely to be completed.

An unsolicited observation of a prior student:

Musings of a Millennial

To introduce myself, I was a student of the author for two years in a small-town high school – history and AP economics. I never had to "try" in high school; I made As and Bs without studying. Then, along came Ward. For the first time, I felt challenged. Dared to think and confronted to be better and, honestly, probably one of the only reasons I made it through college. I contacted him regularly on what to do with certain life situations (and though we haven't always agreed, he has yet to steer me wrong).

Neither of my parents attended college. And though they are amazing people, they are terrible with money, which led to the development of several fears. The largest fear was that, I would graduate high school and be unable to support myself. Liking to help people, but not being able to handle "the blood and guts" of nursing, I reached out to our health teacher. I got the high school to begin a pharmacy technician program – something that would pay higher than minimum wage while trying to support myself through college. (This was during my freshman year and by my junior year, the program was in set in motion and I was able to begin my senior year.)

Our school "acted" as though it was preparing us for college, with information on "how important it was," but not much else. Most meetings and functions focused on how we could meet the required high school credits to graduate. During my sophomore year, after hedging the pathway for the pharmacy technician program, I began looking around. Our small town had very little to offer as far as jobs – fast food, the prison and the hospital, were about your only choices. (I worked at a dry-cleaners through high school.)

Noticing how little the "kids" around me were prepared for life I wondered if the administrators realized, these "kids" were the future of our society - The "kids" that would be making world decisions. This bothered me, a 15-year old, for several weeks. To ease my mind, I emailed the superintendent my thoughts. A few days later, I was pulled from class by the superintendent and brought into the principal's office. They thought the letter I wrote was powerful and wanted to know what I thought would help. Being a kid myself, I wasn't really sure what I could offer as advice other than letting them know that what we had wasn't working. So, I asked what they thought I could do – their response surprised me. They said for me to go to college and come back as a teacher there to help future students. If you're not slapping your knee right now after reading Chapter 2, you need to re-read it. I didn't see the works of this book until after it was mostly finished and I was asked to edit and present my insights, I about fell on the floor. I had never told Ward that story, yet he hit that topic right on the head!

I walked into my junior history class and took my seat like any ordinary Monday. An older man with a grey military cut and stern look on his face walked in and took a seat at the teacher's desk. Where was the little blonde-haired woman that had been teaching us for the last few weeks? Little did I know, this man would shape large parts of my future - from how I handled my finances as an adult, to decisions I made in college and in future jobs.

Our small high school did little to prepare us for the future. Even though Ward was briefly able to give me some tools for college, the truth was, after all the years of being spoon-fed, college was a complete shock. In reference to his "singular paradigm," I was unable to take a textbook, discern and find the key points, often highlighting almost the entire page, or even interpret what I was reading, or to draw conclusions on my own. I was often highlighting entire pages or assuming that the class outline would get me through exams – WRONG. The brief time I had with Ward, probably saved my butt.

Even then, I had a few professors in college that had PowerPoint presentations and that was exactly what was on the exam. Many students simply use e-books or "electronic texts" for school. Why? In my experience, not only is it cheaper, but students can simple look up a word and the word will light up wherever it appears throughout the text – so, simply – you can look up the answers without ever having to read the actual texts. Which made matters worse when I got into "the real world." Don't get me wrong - I worked the entire way through college. However, becoming a financial advisor after graduating was not an easy feat. It bothers me that after a high school and good college education, there were vital skills I lacked to be successful. The exams you must take to be licensed require hours of studying and being able to take what you see in black and white and apply its use in situations. Not just a simple "here's the fact, regurgitate it" scenario, but "here's what you were told, now use it to tell me what happens in this situation." And no, it's not just me – I would say the vast majority, or about 75% I would guess, of my age group that I talk to share the same complaints.

I must also say, the varying education levels from state-to-state are not good. When I was around ten years-old, I moved out of state and was behind in many subjects compared to the students of that state. When I returned two years later to the first state, I was much more advanced and had already covered many subjects. I feel the education system should be standardized across all states, or on the same page, if you will.

These are not issues we should ignore. Many, millennial students feel cheated as they weren't given their best chance. I would hope these ideas will be, at the very least, considered, contemplated and discussed.

Alexys Akey

ABOUT THE AUTHOR

Lawrence "Alan" Ward prides himself on being a Jack of all Trades, Master of None. He began working every summer at the age of 14 then, at 17, left high school to join the Marine Corps. In the Marine Corps, he was a jet mechanic, Instructor, Public Relations Officer, Maintenance Control Chief, Production Control Chief, Maintenance Chief, and Recruiter. After retiring from the USMC he served as a Deputy Sheriff for six years and pursued his Baccalaureate and Master's Degrees in Business; often working 50 hours a week and carrying an academic load of 12 or more hours. His Senior year he stopped work and carried 18-21 hours each semester.

Upon degree completion he became a quality control supervisor in the textile industry and later a manager for a major grocery food chain. During these periods he served as an adjunct instructor for four different Universities in Business and Economics.

He accepted a position in Prison education for the local Community College and later became the department head for the Business, Accounting, Office Systems, and Computer Information Systems Department. After retiring from the CC system he became a History and Economics teacher at the high school level and retired from education. He has since served as an adjunct for one University and two different Community Colleges.

He now enjoys his retirement at Lake Havasu City, Arizona and stays busy writing, fishing, and playing golf. He maintains a blog where he purposely addresses a variety of issues from diverse angles to stimulate discussion. He may be contacted, through his blog, at www.grumpyoldman.net.

"I think, therefore I am."
- Descartes

"I reason and am human. Should I allow anger or prejudice to hamper my reasoning I forfeit a proportional segment of my humanity"
- Ward